REMAINING AND BECOMING

Cultural Crosscurrents in an Hispano School

WITHDRAWI

Shelley Roberts
University of New Mexico

 LAWRENCE ERLBAUM ASSOCIATES, PUBLISHERS
2001   Mahwah, New Jersey   London

Lawrence Erlbaum Associates, Inc., Publishers
10 Industrial Avenue
Mahwah, NJ 07430

Cover design by Kathryn Houghtaling Lacey

Library of Congress Cataloging-in-Publication Data

Roberts, Shelley.
    Remaining and becoming : cultural crosscurrents in an
Hispano school / by Shelley Roberts.
    p. cm.
    Includes bibliographical references and index.
    ISBN 0-8058-2521-5 (cloth : alk. paper)
    ISBN 0-8058-2522-3 (pbk. : alk. paper)
    1. Hispanic-Americans—Education—New Mexico.
    2. Multicultural education—New Mexico.
    3. Hispanic-Americans—New Mexico—Ethnic identity.
    I. Title.
LC2674.N6 R62   2000
371.829'68073—dc21   00-044232
                                                        CIP

Books published by Lawrence Erlbaum Associates are
printed on acid-free paper, and their bindings are chosen
for strength and durability.

Printed in the United States of America
10 9 8 7 6 5 4 3 2 1

For my parents, Carol N. Kinney and Thomas R. Roberts, who raised me to value being part of a community.

For Louis A. Rojas and his family, who forever changed my thinking about remaining and becoming.

Contents

Agradecimientos [Acknowledgments]   xi

Chapter 1   Issues and Contexts: Place, Time, Identity   1

   Finding My Story   7

   A School Within a Community   12

   Terms of Identity: Self-Labeling and Labeling by Others   17

Chapter 2   Souls and Minds: Norteño's Educational History   23

   A Legacy to Reckon With   28

      Spanish Colonization (1598–1821)   28

      Mexican Rule (1821–1848)   30

      United States Occupation (1848–1912)   31

      The Rise of Sectarian Schools: Religion and Culture   34

      The Dixon Case: A Protestant Secular Challenge to Catholic Public   41
      Schools

Chapter 3   People Without a Language: Language Without   50
          a People

   Debate Among Teachers   52

   Debate Among Parents   56

   Debate Epilogue   60

Chapter 4   Caught in the Ebb and Flow of Cultural   62
                Crosscurrents

   Ethnic Identity Versus Ethnic Identification   69

   Cuentos and *Consejos*: Stories and Advice   72

Chapter 5   Domains of Individuality: Public and Private   87

   Luisa: The We of Me   88

   Georgeann: The Links of Common Knowledge   92

   Alfonso: *La Importancia de Saber Dos Idiomas*   94

   Kate: Where Ethnic Pride Ends and Prejudice Begins   97

   Hector: Leave to Make Something of Yourself   99

   Bolívar: Stand and Deliver   104

   A Kaleidoscope of Needs   109

   Teacher Fit   114

Chapter 6   A Fitting School: The Politics of Language   118
                and Identity

   Language Politics: Language as a Problem, Right, Resource   119

      Legislating Language   119

      Forgotten Students: Educational Inequality   121

      Advocacy for Language-Minority Students   123

      Contested Rights About Language   125

   Affirming Ethnicity   126

   Competing Local and National Interests   129

      Barriers to Local Control   129

      A Community School Concept   131

   Ethnic Boundary Maintenance   133

   A Fitting School for Norteño   137

References 143

Appendix   Population Decline of Hispano Villages, 1900–1980   153

Author Index 155

Subject Index 159

Agradecimientos
[Acknowledgments]

Research such as this is an intimate act, and I remain most grateful to my hosts in the school and community, who believed in the worth of my doctoral project and found time in their busy lives to help me understand the needs of these particular students growing up in this particular community. The promise of confidentiality restrains my listing you by name, but I hope the story I tell on these pages will do justice to your trust in me. Perhaps my most cherished learning experiences came from your generous hospitality as we chatted over a bowl of red chili with fresh tortillas, or a *cafecito*. Having those of you in Norteño read drafts of my manuscript gives me confidence about how the story will play in Norteño. There are many stories to be told in Norteño, your pseudonym, and this is but one. I continue to urge you to write your own stories.

In this story the readers meet Bolívar, Norteño's equivalent to Jaime Escalante in the movie *Stand and Deliver*. Bolívar's own story of becoming educated and being an educator tells us a lot about growing up in Northern New Mexico then and now. Using money he received from an award for excellence in teaching, Bolívar established a college scholarship for students pursuing math and science. All royalties from this book will be contributed to this fund in recognition of the kind of vision Bolívar has about who these students are and can become.

Writing about research involves as much assistance as the actual research does. No amount of gratitude is enough for the two men in my life—my loving husband, Dewey Moore, and my caring mentor, Alan Peshkin—who kept reassuring me that I could tell this story. My other dissertation committee members—Georgia García, Betty Merchant, Philip Zodhiates—brought to the project their own multicultural biographies.

Their commitment to multicultural education encouraged me, and their individual perspectives brought new dimensions to my research. Special thanks go to Kay Tenorio at the University of New Mexico for introducing Alan Peshkin and me to this research site, the Louis Rojas family for furnishing my temporary home, and Marleen Pugach for helping me learn the publication ropes. Carolyn Atkins from the Menaul Historical Society in Albuquerque and researcher Deborah Norman provided much direction as I sorted through the history of Presbyterian mission schools in Northern New Mexico. The Parent–Faculty Organization of the University of Illinois Laboratory High School, where I was the director/principal when beginning this book, gave me an airplane ticket to New Mexico to complete my research. And let me not forget the hand that fed. The cost of long-term, immersion research would have been prohibitive without the generous support of the Spencer Foundation.

Converting my dissertation to a book occurred thanks to the generous gift of collegial reading from reviewer Ursula Casanova at Arizona State University, Ann Nihlen at the University of New Mexico, and students in my qualitative research methods courses, especially Susan Lloyd and Kim Potowski. At Lawrence Erlbaum, I am indebted to Naomi Silverman's patience with the slow transformation of my dissertation into a book, to Jane Woychick's copyediting ability that anticipated the needs of my readers, and to Sarah Wahlert for getting this book into circulation.

To my families in New Mexico and in the Midwest, thank you for all the encouragement and sacrifice involved in living with and apart from an ethnographic researcher.

1

Issues and Contexts: Place, Time, Identity

Education challenged the villagers to not remain isolated, to become more aware of the outside world, and to become professionals. Education continues this challenge to not remain in Norteño,[1] but education is now looking backwards at the cost of becoming. What remains of the past?

> —From an interview with a Norteño *anciano*

"I am the only American here." With these few words, a New York Presbyterian missionary differentiated herself in 1889 from Catholic, Spanish-speaking people who wrested a living from their remote territorial environment in Northern New Mexico. By doing so, she struck at the core of Norteño identity, endorsing an American Protestant cultural standard that would nag at Norteño tradition. The history of the Norteño School District, a pseudonym, is embedded in the 200-year history of its community and a several-centuries-longer Hispano history in the region. It is a public school district, not fully consolidated until 1972, in which Catholics battled Protestants for the souls of the children, in which Catholic nuns and priests were employed as teachers until 1949.

The ebb and flow of cultural crosscurrents in Northern New Mexico add richness and complexity to the educational issues the Norteño community faces. Spain, Mexico, and the United States—each has claimed sovereignty over the region with different goals for and attitudes about

---

[1]*Norteño* [Northern] is the Spanish term often used to refer to Northern New Mexico, which was the northern most outpost of the Spanish empire in the New World. *Norteños* [Northerners] are Spanish-heritage residents whose ancestors settled in the region during the 17th and 18th centuries. I use the term Norteño as a pseudonym for my research community in Northern New Mexico.

the welfare of the people. The coming of public education to the Norteño region is a story of contested purposes. Out of this unusual history came the rise of sectarian schools, litigation for secular schools, consolidation, and finally local control. The contemporary story of education in Norteño reflects how the people are dealing with the political, religious, and cultural history of the region. Norteños—a minority in the outside world but a majority in their own world—are debating how the functions of the school should respond to changes introduced by outside cultural influences.

The Norteño School District today consists of a K–12 campus that serves 14 highland villages covering almost 500 square miles, each with an average population of 150 persons. The district, which is among New Mexico's most rurally isolated school systems, is now run by Hispanos, an ethnic group whose regional presence dates back to the Spanish colonization of Northern New Mexico in the 17th century. The modern school campus is a contrast to the educational options most parents and grandparents knew; which included village public schools, a parochial day school in Norteño, Protestant boarding schools in Santa Fe and Albuquerque, and Indian boarding schools in Santa Fe. The role of schooling in Norteño has changed significantly during the past three generations, and today's circumstances reflect the cultural crosscurrents that have flowed through the community. As the community changes, the cultural patterns change.

This book is not an inventory of cultural traits meant to measure the continuity of cultural tradition; nor is it a historical ethnography of literacy or an ethnohistory of ethnicity.[2] It is an analysis about the ambiguity of education: the losses and gains that education brings and what future it can and should serve. It is about asking, Is what the students

---

[2]For an analysis of the social context of literacy in colonial New Mexico that includes student perspectives about instruction, read the dissertation *Literacy, Schooling, and Society in Colonial New Mexico: 1692–1821* by Bernardo Phillip Gallegos (1988). Gallegos considered formal and informal literacy instruction and literacy's relationship to personal and collective efficacy and activism. His historical ethnography of literacy included "material conditions, motivations, opportunities, needs and demands, traditions, and transformations ... linguistic forms, dialects, communication channels and networks, pushes and pulls from religion, culture, politics, the economy, etc." (pp. 20–21). For an analysis of ethnicity in an ethnohistorical context, see Adrian Herminio Bustamante's dissertation *Los Hispanos: Ethnicity and Social Change in New Mexico* (1982). This study focused on the ethnicity and ethnic labeling used by the Hispanos of Northern New Mexico during five time periods: the Spanish Period (1692–1821), the Mexican Period (1821–1846), the American Territorial Period (1846–1912), the Assimilation Period (1912–1976), and the Contemporary Period (1977–1982).

are learning worth as much as what they are forgetting?[3] This book deals with the politics of identity and the concept of boundaries during a time of rapid change.

The terms *remaining* and *becoming* in the book's title refer to the goals of Norteños, both those who seek change and those who want to stop it from occurring. There is a sense of urgency in both groups, and from this urgency, debates ensue about whether or not Norteño schools should teach the local culture and language. By *remaining,* I mean what a school does or hopes to do in the name of what it sees as the heritage of the students it serves. By *becoming,* I mean what a school does or hopes to do in the name of change.

The conflicting loyalties of religion and culture are woven into this story of remaining and becoming, as are the cornerstones of Norteño society—family, faith, land, and language.[4] By exploring historical factors and ideologies of a particular school within a particular community, my hope is to understand community expectations for the school as a fitting place for their children. The choices, contingencies, and options open to students are contextualized within the intersection of their own life histories, their school and community histories, and contemporary circumstances of social change (Kimball & Partridge, 1979). My goal is not to generalize necessarily from the particular to the universal, but to join others in suggesting that we get away from discussing students in a generic sense and move toward looking at them in relation to the communities in which they live (Donato, 1999; Peshkin, 1991; Spindler, 1982). The ethnic composition of the community, the community's settlement pattern, changing lifestyles of the community, the way education came to the community, who controls the schools, being a community of faith, being a poor school district—How do these all shape what becoming educated means in this Hispano community in Northern New Mexico?

This ethnography represents one of four fieldwork projects coordinated by Alan Peshkin, currently at Stanford University, that explored

---

[3]Cheikh Hamidou Kane (1963) talked about the problem of education for the African being "Europeanized" in *Ambiguous Adventure*: "The adventure thus describes the movement from a oneness of things, a sense of totality in that oneness to the possibility of twoness, the possibility which only brings with it ambiguities and a 'nonness' in the twoness" (p. xvi). W. E. B. DuBois (1969) also wrote of this "twoness" in *The Souls of Black Folk*: "One ever feels his twoness ... two souls, two thoughts, two unreconciled strivings; two warring ideals in one dark body" (p. 45).

[4]Deborah Melendy Norman (1993) referred to these four cornerstones of village culture in a presentation titled "Northern New Mexico: The Role of Religious Belief in Cultural Preservation." She is conducting research on the role that religious beliefs and practices have played in maintaining the integrity of the Norteño culture.

school–community relationships within four major culture groups in New Mexico: Indian, Mexican, Hispano, and Anglo. Peshkin organized the research in the Indian and Anglo high schools, and Marleen Pugach of the University of Wisconsin at Milwaukee organized the research in the Mexican high school. Having grown up in Northern New Mexico, I chose the Hispano project. Although each book is intended to stand alone, Peshkin (1997) has stated:

> Together the four studies form a portrait of schooling in New Mexico, perhaps similar to that in many other places as well ... [T]hey document the range of ways that host communities in our educationally decentralized society use the prerogatives of local control to "create" schools that fit local cultural inclinations.

> I think of the Indian, Hispano, Mexican, and Anglo studies as explorations of the interactions between cultural *remaining*, as reflected in the students' traditions of home and community, and cultural *becoming*, as encouraged by the students' experiences in schools that historically have been established as agents of Anglo-American society. At best, there may be some tension in the generational differences between what children anywhere learn at school, and what their parents know and value. Such differences may embody disputed orientations between young and old about the substance of remaining and becoming. At worst, strain, confusion, and ambiguity may be generated by home–school and community–society orientations that are separated by a vast cultural divide. (p. xi)[5]

My initial familiarity with Hispanos came through my own schooling experience during the 1950s and 1960s in Los Alamos, the site of a national scientific laboratory placed in remote Northern New Mexico during World War II. Although housing was scarce, some Hispano employees of the national laboratory chose to have a second home in Los Alamos to take advantage of industrial jobs and the federally funded school system. Hispano classmates' families often commuted back to the villages on the weekends. Most villagers recruited as school custodians and bus drivers did not bring their families to Los Alamos but lived in school district dormitories during the week. Government-owned housing mixed the few

---

[5]Peshkin introduced the four-book Lawrence Erlbaum series in the preface of *Places of Memory: Whiteman's Schools and Native American Communities* (1997). Other books in the series are *On the Border of Opportunity: Education, Community, and Language at the U.S.–Mexico Line* by Marleen C. Pugach (1998) and *Permissible Advantage? The Moral Consequences of Elite Schooling* by Alan Peshkin (2000).

families from the villages with those of us who migrated from other parts of the country. Although mingling occurred, I remained four times removed from these Hispanos by virtue of my social class, ethnicity, religion, and midwestern family roots.

The origins of this research project date back to two epiphanies in the 1970s: my marriage to a Mexican-American classmate from Los Alamos and a summer farming with him near Norteño. Both experiences opened my eyes to educational inequalities in the region and to realities of classmates from the villages, who grew up between two cultural worlds. Although once separated from Hispano history by a wide valley and from Mexican-American history by family origins, my marital choice and budding interest in educational anthropology drew me into the complex ethnic relationships in Northern New Mexico. I can relate to the anxiety of "betweenness"—not always identifying with the culture I am identified with and identifying with cultures that constantly remind me that I am different.

Being a native of Northern New Mexico with some fluency in Spanish did not guarantee me credibility with Norteños. A succession of social scientists had plowed this cultural turf before me, turning up images of village life viewed by some as stereotypical and negative (Paredes, 1978). The Norteños' persisting perception of Anglo exploitation and misrepresentation instructed me about where this community drew ethnic boundaries. When I presented my research at a Norteño teachers' in-service sponsored by Northern New Mexico Community College, the Hispano writing instructor rejected my study saying, "Why not study Los Alamos, where you're from?"

Los Alamos is my story, but it is also part of their story of remaining and becoming. This scientific community, born out of the Atomic Age in the 1940s, dropped an "Anglo bomb" on Norteños and set in motion an accelerated pace of change in their lives. New employment opportunities meant economic survival to the villages; today Hispanics (mostly Hispanos) represent 28% of the workforce at the Los Alamos National Laboratories, and many of them can now commute daily on the new four-lane highway up the mesa (Padilla, 1994). The proximity of Anglo culture joined two powerful and conflicting systems of socialization for Norteños. They are characterized as "this is how you were raised" and "this is how you should be." Growing up in Northern New Mexico, I have come to understand the homogenizing power of the Anglo culture and the resentment of those who called me *gabacha,* a foreigner. The story of

Los Alamos waits to be told from the Hispano perspective, as well as from mine and that of others.[6]

The Hispano writing instructor also raised concerns about the trade-off between confidentiality and accountability. "If you use pseudonyms for the school and the characters in the book and change identifying characteristics or situational details, how would our school get the recognition it deserves and how would we know you did not just make it all up?" Taking his pride and distrust to heart, I am nevertheless constrained by the terms of anonymity under which I received permission to do the study—a precaution by the school district's superintendent and a protection for the participants, who will go on living in Norteño long after I leave. The impact of my words and perspective remains an issue. Thus, to be true to Norteño views without jeopardizing community relationships stands as my greatest challenge. Only my behavior in the community, the words I write about it, and my response to Norteño residents' critiques of my manuscript drafts might assure them that I came not as an evaluator, but as a learner to see the school from their perspective.

I mention these negative reactions to my presence in order to keep them in mind as I write, as well as to acknowledge them to others. I heard Norteños refer to themselves as conquered or oppressed people. I heard painful stories of resentment about Anglos who make money from books about Norteño lives. I heard sentiments of regret when they talked about the *vendidos*—those who sold land to the Anglos and thereby let outsiders into the Norteño world. According to one Norteño with a passionate concern about the future, "Traditional people from Northern New Mexico have always believed that they don't inherit the land from their parents; they simply have borrowed it from their children." These feelings became part of my research context, because they are part of the older generation's message to their children about who they are and who their children should become.

Living in a community involves maintaining relationships, which sometimes limits what people say to each other. As an outsider, I prompted opinions and frustrations that were not ordinarily included in the community's

---

[6]Six months after the writing in-service, I read about a study being conducted by the University of New Mexico Oral History Program on the impact of Los Alamos on the personal, familial, and community lives of Northern New Mexicans. The interview project, directed by Dr. Carlos Vásquez, was timed to coincide with the Los Alamos National Laboratory's 50th anniversary. See "Oral History Program Examines Impact of Los Alamos National Lab on *Paisanos*: Land Abandoned for Lab Security" in *arellano* magazine, Winter 1993–1994.

conversation about its aspirations for its children. Community members expressed their sense of multiple realities and intense ideological debates provoked by living in a cultural borderland (Anzaldúa, 1987).[7]

This text includes both my voice and community voices, all of which I view as partial and incomplete. I reject the notion of detached research, for I have affected the conversations I entered, and these conversations have affected me. The act of questioning shaped the act of meaning people gave to their stories of compelling motives, strong feelings, vague aspirations, clear intentions, or well-defined goals:

> There is no fixed meaning in the past, for with each new telling the context varies, the audience differs, the story is modified, and ... 'retellings become foretellings.' We continually discover new meanings. All of us ... must accept responsibility for understanding society as told and retold. (Turner & Bruner, 1986, p. 153)

In Norteño, I endeavored to enter and to get the gist of a conversation that began long before I arrived and that will continue long after I leave. Thus, this is not a definitive story of Norteño School District; there can be no such story. Instead, I hope to portray how influences from outside and from within the community shape the promise and the reality of becoming and remaining for the young people in Norteño today.[8]

FINDING MY STORY

In Norteño, belonging counts. A candidate's board of education election campaign flyer listed his educational and professional qualifications and then informed voters that "I have been a resident of Norteño for over five years, but my family roots in the community date back over 200 years." Norteño consists of those who never left, those who returned, those who visit, and the void left by those who never came back (see Appendix). How does the Norteño School District view the needs of their students, some of whom will stay, others of whom will leave?

---

[7]In *Borderlands, La Frontera: The New Mestiza*, Gloria Anzaldúa (1987) portrayed how people of mixed ancestry develop a tolerance for contradictions and ambiguity in the crossroads between cultures.

[8]In *Culture and Truth: The Remaking of Social Analysis*, anthropologist Renato Rosaldo (1989) used Kenneth Burke's parable of the endless conversation to illustrate the enduring character of society that exists before, during, and after our lifetimes. This conversation embodies conflict and change, taking the form of challenge and response to structures that shape lives over time. Social analysts consider the interplay of *structure* and *agency* as a central issue in social theory—how received structures shape human conduct and how human conduct alters received structures (p. 104).

Eighty-nine percent of the students and nearly 80% of the teachers are Hispanos; approximately 75% of the Norteño School District employees are Norteño natives.[9] The seven board of education members, all Norteño High School alumni, bring to their monthly deliberations diverse professional backgrounds—education, armed services, computers, engineering, criminology. Many school board members left the community, became educated, and returned. They thought they were coming back to resume life in the traditional Hispano culture they had left behind, but they inevitably brought change back with them. They do not always agree about what becoming educated can and should mean to the students of Norteño.

The Norteño school district leaders who were part of this study came of age during the 1960s, when minorities across the United States began rejecting cultural labels that implied deprivation and demanding that society respect those attributes that make minorities different, not deviant. Although few Norteño educators describe themselves as activists, the civil rights fervor of the 1960s put into motion events that significantly changed how the Norteño School District developed from that point on. The schools in this region, long neglected by the outside world, finally began to receive attention: an equalized state funding formula, federal assistance for low-income families and underachieving students, bilingual education, and affirmative action.

The Norteño School District now carries a statewide reputation for being successful. The school boasts of alumni who are doctors, professors, nuclear physicists, and engineers. The *1990 Census of Population and Housing* indicates that 58% of Norteño residents 25 years old and older have high school degrees, and close to 9% have at least a bachelor's degree (U.S. Department of Commerce, 1992b). But 25% who enroll in seventh grade never graduate.

In the 10 months of the 1992–93 academic year that I lived in Norteño, I participated broadly in school and community events. I explored the critical issues that arose in Norteño as the walls of relative isolation, ethnic homogeneity, and stability began to break down as a result of the incursions of the non-Hispano, outside world. From within the rhythms of

---

[9]According to the narrative of Norteño's 1993 proposal for a transitional bilingual math and science program in Grades 7–12, the student population for the Norteño School District is 89% Hispanic, 4% Native American, and 7% Anglo. The staff population (including administrators, maintenance personnel, clerical and cafeteria workers, and bus contractors) is 90% Hispanic, 4% Native American, and 6% Anglo.

daily life, I observed how people prioritized their lives. Through their interactions—or lack thereof—I saw changing values and beliefs in action. To examine the historical context of the community, I looked for cultural, political, and economic factors that have affected how Norteño schools developed. Three Norteño superintendents, having 30 years of experience among them, provided an overview of how the school district has developed. I interviewed *ancianos*—the elders—and parents to compare how they grew up with how young people are growing up today. The several families who provided me with three-generation accounts made clear the continuity and change in identity, beliefs, values, and hopes. Archival research expanded their stories of how the school and community have changed, each affecting the other.

Everyone talked of change. I probed to uncover its substance, and, most important, its impact on the lives of the students. Throughout my year of visiting K–12 classes at school and living in the community, I listened to the young people describe themselves and the messages they receive from within and beyond Norteño. I watched them on and off campus, in church, and in their homes. I interviewed secondary students alone or with friends. I was curious about the expectations of peers, family, teachers, and the community regarding the students' place in American society. I tried to make sense of the multitude of expectations that affect the students' sense of identity and vision of future possibilities.

The focus of this book is on schooling for Hispano students, but I also interviewed the two Indian students from a neighboring pueblo who chose to attend Norteño High School rather than board at the Santa Fe Indian School for their secondary education. Their pueblo's existence precedes the Norteño community's, and many cultural traits Hispanos associate with remaining can be traced back to pueblo traditions. In addition, I spoke with Anglo students whose families came to Norteño as merchants several generations ago or as hippies when the commune movement reached Northern New Mexico at the end of the 1960s.[10] These students talked of the friction and unease they feel when crossing the boundaries between their family, peer, and school worlds and explained how the cultural incongruity between these three social worlds affects their self-perception. Each developed adaptation strategies to move between their different home and school environments (Phelan,

---

[10]In New Mexico, the term *Anglo* originally referred to an English-speaking, White person coming into New Mexico from the eastern and middle-western states. Nowadays, the term is used for any non-Indo-Hispanic American (Cobos, 1983, p. 10).

Davidson, & Yu, 1998). As the school has become more multicultural, it has had to deal with increasingly diverse expectations about schooling. My focus on the Hispano students should not be interpreted as the sole concern of the teachers, many of whom I observed extending sensitivity and encouragement to all their students.

My research considers how a community feels about generational changes in the continuous process of learning to be or to become something or someone (Wolcott, 1987).[11] The promise and substance of being and becoming in a particular place, time, and setting are neither easy to talk about nor to recognize. I attended carefully to the messages the students received in different school and community settings. I asked older students what they thought their teachers were trying to communicate to them besides the content of the course; what their parents were trying to impress upon them, and how other significant people in their lives were trying to influence them.

Native teachers and those who came to Norteño from as far away as the East Coast described the messages they try to send to students. I asked, "What should these students understand about themselves and the outside world before they leave here?" Depending on what the teachers consider to be missing in the lives of young people, their messages to students are from the community's history or from the world outside Norteño. For example, one high school teacher emphasizes current events and geography to compensate for the lack of exposure students have to the outside world; another creates an intergenerational oral history project to expose students to the history of their world. The needs the teachers identified often stemmed directly from their own biographies. One native teacher wants his students never to face the embarrassment he encountered when he arrived at college unprepared to compete with Anglos.

While trying to understand how students sort out all the messages they hear about who they are and can become, I discovered how diverse these messages are. Debates on the school grounds and in the community about whether or not to define the school district as bilingual brought out a wide range of opinions about the role of language in relation to remaining and becoming. The generational shift in dominant language preference from Spanish to English concerns those who argue

---

[11]In "The Anthropology of Learning," Harry Wolcott (1987) distinguished between educational research that focuses on learning per se and contextualized, culturally oriented accounts of learning to be or become something or someone.

that the schools should sustain the heritage of the students' home culture. Others advocate exposing students to the outside world as much as possible and emphasizing English to enhance the students' competitive edge.

The school district's debate about bilingual education brings into question the role of the school in helping the community deal with the outside world. Given the community's cultural and socioeconomic profile, should the Norteño School District help minimize or maximize the community's uniqueness, or should it try to do some of each? If the school district defines itself as bilingual, will it be going backward or forward?

I heard opinions about bilingual education in formal and informal settings: the chambers of the board of education, faculty meetings, parent advisory council meetings, bilingual conferences, in-services, faculty lounges, living rooms, restaurants, and churches. Whether proponents of remaining or of becoming, all want to instill in their children a strong sense of Norteño place and identity, but they disagree about whether the families or the school should be responsible for such socialization.

Some argue that the school should be concerned with the possible disappearance of the Spanish associated with the region. The more radical propose that their colloquial Spanish be taught as a defense against the encroachment of the Anglo world. Others want a rigorous school curriculum that exposes students to the world beyond their valley. Moderates take a more pragmatic approach: Bilingual education provides needed resources in the form of government grants that cannot be garnered any other way by the school district.

The bilingual debate divides students. They feel caught between the competing claims of two cultural worlds that continue to shape who they are learning to be. Changing cultural tides pull at their sense of being an Hispano and an American. They disagree about pressures for linguistic loyalty and being labeled "the last hope" for their culture.

Most Norteño adolescents seem curiously unconcerned about their ethnicity—a matter of considerable controversy among community educators and other adults. The Norteño experience once meant living within the local culture, more or less isolated from mainstream America. Today it means living between and sometimes outside of two cultures, separated geographically from the mainstream and linguistically from the local culture. I talked with young and old people about the complexity of living in dual cultural worlds. Ethnicity appears to be a more salient issue in the lives of adults. Only adolescents who have spent time living away from Norteño have thought much about their own ethnic identity.

Norteño's bilingual debate reflects the identity politics occurring throughout Northern New Mexico. Hispanos fear that their culture could be lost with the increasing presence of Anglo society eroding Hispanos' cultural, political, and economic strength. For some, slowing the tide of cultural change means putting up barriers. Resistance to assimilation has taken on various forms—land grant claims, water rights disputes, lobbying for more access to surrounding national forests, protests against economic development, and refusal to sell land to outsiders. A mandate that schools teach the regional culture and language could become another barrier.

How ironic that the seeming timelessness of Norteño cannot camouflage the urgency felt by those who want the schools to stop the accelerating rush toward the ways of the outside world. The interactions between the Norteño and Anglo cultures have brought socioeconomic mobility to many villagers. Affirmative action, state equalization formulas, federal programs for low-income families, and bilingual education have enhanced becoming. But the movement to reverse assimilation puts a positive spin on "dissimilation"—the renewal of ethnicity (Yinger, 1981). Norteños today disagree about whether advantage arises out of their conformity with or difference from Anglos.

A SCHOOL WITHIN A COMMUNITY

In Norteño School District, the elevation exceeds the population. In many ways, Norteño is still extremely isolated. The mountains that surround it interfere with radio broadcasts from regional stations and also make roads uninviting during winter. There is no local newspaper to track the pulse of the community, but a weekly regional paper places what happens in Norteño within the broader context of Northern New Mexico. Besides the daily school bulletin and the weekly church bulletin, people can only depend on an informal process of talk in public places and chance encounters to find out what is going on.

The school grounds are surrounded by Indian reservation land, fallow fields, the Forest Service department, and a *morada*. *Moradas* are places of worship for the *Penitentes*, male members of a lay religious organization related to the Roman Catholic Church.[12] *Moradas* often serve as centers of cultural activity and community action. In the small *camposanto* [cemetery] behind the *morada*, graves are marked by decorated crosses, ornate signs that greet deceased dads and moms, and American flags that honor veterans. Because the villages are not incorporated, some families have their own cemeteries scattered throughout the valley. Some villages have separate cemeteries for Protestants and Catholics.

Yellow school buses follow their early morning routes past scattered mobile homes and tin-roofed adobes to gather 800 children from clusters of mountain villages. Navigating the back roads and highways takes most bus drivers about an hour. I ride a bus one autumn morning to learn about the children the bus driver picks up and their rural communities. Along a dirt road, we stop to pick up 7-year-old Diego, who is accompanied by his grandmother. Diego lives with his grandparents because his mother left the region to find work. The bus driver laments that the large families of the parents' generation are a thing of the past.

Two stylish eighth graders seated in the back are comparing weekend exploits on their three-wheelers. Arnold wears Nike high-tops, a Bulls cap, and a T-shirt with a motto: "Individuality is not a one-way street. It's a freeway." We stop to wait for stragglers, and I spot a large foundation next to a basketball court, the only remains of the village school built by the Works Project Administration during the Great Depression. Antonia and Denise, both with long hair and spiked bangs, board the bus and inform the driver they will be staying after school. Antonia belongs to the high school drill team, and Denise is one of 24 high school students participating in a job training program and placement service for academically at-risk students (JTPA). Jane, the teenage daughter of 1970s hippies, sits alone and reads. Acceptance does not come easily in this community for her and other hippie offspring.

Around a corner, we slow down to pass an octogenarian who prefers to travel in his horse-drawn wagon. Jesús takes pride in not being dependent

---

[12]Sometime during the late 18th century, a religious force known as *Penitentes* [Brotherhood of Our Father Jesus] emerged among the Spanish pioneers in Northern New Mexico. Due to isolation and lack of priests, this folk religion evolved to take care of the religious and social needs of the villages. The *Penitentes* acquired considerable political influence and have long played an appreciable role in the history of the region. In recent years, Archbishop Sanchez was instrumental in uniting the *moradas*. Their aging ranks are benefiting from a resurgence of faith among the younger men of the villages. *Penitentes* resent what outsiders have written about them, but more information is available in Marta Weigle's book, *Brothers of Light, Brothers of Blood* (1976).

on a car. However, he could not resist a bit of modernization: He replaced the old wooden wagon wheels with rubber tires. Before automobiles became common, Jesús took 2 days to travel to Taos, the nearest large town. Today, his sons take 30 minutes to cover this distance.

As the bus bumps along narrow back roads, the driver points to the land granted by the king of Spain to settlers centuries before: "Dividing property equally among children over the generations has left most of us with too little land to make a living." Patchwork property lines carve up the villages into small plots. Abandoned adobe homesteads are markers of possession for absent owners. We see a few horses and cows feeding. Assorted vehicles and farm equipment are parked in front of the homes; behind the buildings are small fields of corn, beans, or alfalfa. A cultural landscape has been impressed upon the natural environment: Homemade signs lean against gates, advertising hay, apples, *piñón* [pine nuts], and *chicos* [dried corn] for sale.

Acequias (community irrigation ditches) wind through the valleys, waiting their turn to carry water to the fields. No longer the critical issue it was when agriculture was predominant, water remains the resource that organizes community life. The driver explains how each village has an acequia commission headed by a *mayordomo*, who is responsible for delegating the irrigation ditch upkeep tasks and water to the farmers. *Mayordomos* are stewards responsible for the maintenance of community property. In a book about his *mayordomo* experience, Stanley Crawford, an Anglo, wrote, "Next to blood relationships, which rule the valley, come water relationships. The arteries of ditches and bloodlines [channeled centuries ago] cut across each other in patterns of astounding complexity" (1988, pp. 23–24).

Passing by houses crowded along the road and surrounded by the limitless space of the mountains, I recall how a board of education member had described the families in the district differently than the bus driver did: land rich, cash poor. According to the 1990 census, the per capita income in Norteño is about $7,000, and 30% of the Norteños live below the poverty level (U.S. Department of Commerce, 1992b). School enrollment data indicate 78% of the students live in low-income families. A fundamental change in village economy came with the shift from bartering to buying in the early part of the 20th century. More recently, when a nearby mineral mine, the county's largest employer, reduced its workforce, more Norteño workers shifted to low-paying jobs and to welfare programs (see Table 1.1).

TABLE 1.1

Occupation Profile of Norteño School District Families

Occupation	Father	Mother
Unemployed/welfare	21.6%	9.9%
Farmer/rancher	11.4%	4.4%
Farmer/unskilled labor	15.9%	7.7%
Skilled labor	18.2%	4.4%
Small business	6.8%	8.8%
Technician	2.3%	N/A
Retired worker	6.8%	3.3%
Other	17.0%	59.3%

Note. Adapted from Norteño School District 1993 Transitional Bilingual Education Proposal for Jr./Sr. Math and Science, p. 7.

Locals covet school bus contracts, for there are only three major employers in Norteño: the school district, the highway department, and the forest service. Fifty-six percent of the county jobs are dependent on skiing and tourism. In the village, several families operate general stores and gas stations, but most workers commute at least 60 miles to their city jobs. Retired people live in many of the homes, and a good number of families depend on disability entitlements due to labor injuries.

Nevertheless, the villages appear more prosperous than when I lived nearby 20 years ago. I see some passive solar homes, Cherokee jeeps, video stores, more gas stations, several food stores, and better roads. But the bus driver disagrees, telling me that young couples cannot afford to build a home. Instead, they renovate old family homesteads or put trailer houses on inherited land that has been subdivided many times before.

Outside the Catholic Church, the parish *mayordomo* has put up a bilingual message on the new signboard next to the road: "Good luck students. Cast all your cares on God! That anchor holds." And for many it does. The Catholic Church remains the center of community life for 90% of the residents, with mass scheduled daily and prayer meetings, communion classes, and support groups gathering during the week. Vatican II reforms have changed the expression of faith in the community, allowing homilies in Spanish and English and lay participation in the services.

Once a week the church's bus, marked by scripture painted on its side, stops at the elementary school at the end of the day to pick up children for religion classes.

Pockets of people hang out at the local café where the bus driver and I finish up with a cup of coffee. She greets another customer affectionately as *"Compadre"* [godfather].[13] The bonds of *compadres* extend beyond village limits and kin to maintain a sense of "regional community" (Deutsch, 1987, p. 12).[14] Old-timers sip coffee and speak in the local Spanish, and younger men tend to speak Spanglish, or *mocho*—a combination of Spanish and English. Two little girls talk in English, with a sprinkling of Spanish. The young people, some of whom have grown up with Spanish-speaking grandparents and others, are used to hearing Spanish and to receiving instructions around the house in Spanish.

Returning home from school, my neighbor drives by and raises his index finger from the steering wheel to wave. Parading elk antlers on his pickup's front hood, he pulls off to offer elk pelts to a shop owner who sells flies for fishing. Truckloads full of firewood, *la leña*, go by as people prepare for the winter. "Woodcutting is ... a stubborn adherence to form, the ritualization of subsistence," which contributes to the Norteño sense of identity and belonging (Sagel, 1992, p. 15). Woodcutting, hunting, and fishing are part of the Norteño character—*Somos gente de la tierra* [We are people of the earth]—a paradoxical image when juxtaposed with the ubiquitous material culture of late 20th-century America.

When I stop for an errand, the storekeeper introduces himself to me as a native New Mexican: "If you scratch the dirt under this house, you'll find almost 300 years of my ancestors' roots and blood." Land and blood relationships define identity: Where are you from? identifies by Spanish colonial subculture; Who are your parents? identifies by family line. The lengthy legacy of Norteño Hispanos distinguishes them from more recent Spanish-speaking immigrants. The Norteños' identities are shaped by the sense of a homeland from which they have drawn nourishment for centuries. Their strong sense of place has been shaped and reshaped by

---

[13]Catholic parents designate godparents at the baptisms and weddings of their children. The relationship created between the parents and godparents is considered to be as important as family ties. The Hispano tradition is to address godparents as *comadre* or *compadre*, rather than by their names.

[14]Sarah Deutsch (1987) used the notion of "regional community" as a framework to examine the nature and ramifications of the intersection of Anglo-Hispanic cultures, class, and gender in Northern New Mexico villages from the territorial period to the beginning of World War II. See *No Separate Refuge: Culture, Class, and Gender on an Anglo-Hispanic Frontier in the American Southwest, 1880–1940*.

the colonial land grants passed down through the families, the Old World model of *plazas* [community] and stewardship, relative isolation in their particular natural and cultural environments, and gradual intermarriage with Pueblo and nomad Indians. Norteños are inheritors of a particular landscape—the "emotional geography that shapes the lives and the character of the people who live there" (Warren, 1987, p. 54).

TERMS OF IDENTITY:
SELF-LABELING AND LABELING BY OTHERS

The surge of activism among the Spanish speakers in the Southwest has complicated the choice of names by which they are known and has also made it clear that they wish to choose the name by which they are known. In years past the Anglo-Americans used whatever term they chose, depending on the attitude of those who bestowed the name. That is not so today. Some have decided to be known as Mexican Americans, others as Chicanos, and the old colonials in New Mexico as Spanish Americans or as Hispanos.

—Campa (1979, p. 5)

Ethnic self-labeling and labeling by others has changed over the centuries for Spanish-speaking inhabitants in the American Southwest. For more than 200 years, during the period of Spanish colonialism, New World Spanish settlers were called *españoles mejicanos* [Spanish Mexicans], a term that designated the province where the subjects of the Spanish crown originated. A complex rubric of ethnic labels classified the regional population by race and nationality. Many of the earliest colonists going to Northern New Mexico were Spaniards who were *peninsulares* [born in Spain] or *criollos* [born in New Spain]. Other colonists were *mestizos*—offspring of Spanish and Indian miscegenation in New Spain. Given the settlement pattern of sending mostly men to the Spanish northland, mating with the indigenous women produced a mixed gene pool and hybrid cultures. Colonial society was stratified with *peninsulares* and elite *criollos* at the top and unacculturated Indians at the bottom; *castas* [mixed blood] were ordered in between according to how mixed and how hispanicized they were (Bustamante, 1982; Campa, 1977).

Although many Spanish-speaking people in Northern New Mexico may not identify themselves as Indians, for many their origins trace back to the *genízaros*. The *genízaros* were nomadic and non-pueblo captive Indians "transculturated" according to the guidelines in the *Recopilación de leyes de los reynos de las indias* and used by the Spaniards to defend the Hispanic Catholic frontier. Through a civil process of *reducción*, the *genízaros* were transformed religiously, culturally, linguistically, and socially into Hispanic citizens, or *vecinos* (Córdova, 1979).[15]

During the territorial period, *The New Mexican* newspaper distinguished *Mexicans* from *Americans*, and the Hispano-controlled newspapers coined the term *neo mexicano* during the mid-1880s. *La Voz del Pueblo*, a Spanish-language newspaper, introduced the term *hispano americano* by the end of the 1890s (Bustamante, 1982). The importance of being "Spanish" in 20th-century New Mexico comes from not wanting to be considered Mexican. Several authors have traced the increased use of the term *Hispano* back to the period when large numbers of Mexicans immigrated to New Mexico after the Mexican Revolution (1910). By emphasizing direct descent from the Spanish colonists, "Spanish Americans" hoped to separate themselves from the Anglo color consciousness and racism directed at the Mexicans (Bustamante, 1982; Campa, 1977; Deutsch, 1987; González, 1967; Stoddard, 1973). Their lighter complexions, European heritage, and American citizenship allowed Hispanos to better their economic and, in some cases, their social status. As a display of patriotism, the *Alianza Hispano-Americana* staged a DeVargas pageant in Santa Fe on the Fourth of July in 1911 and 1912 to commemorate the Spanish reconquest of New Mexico (Wilson, 1997).[16]

In the early 1950s, Arthur Campa conducted a lexical investigation of the Northern New Mexican Spanish language, asking in both Spanish and English about ethnic terms the natives preferred to use for themselves. When asked in Spanish what term they used to designate a native Spanish-speaking New Mexican, they answered without exception, "*Mexicano.*" Later, when asked the same question in English, they invariably answered, "Spanish American." They referred to an individual from Mexico as a *Mexicano de México* in Spanish and as a *Mexican* in English. Campa (1979) drew several inferences from this investigation:

---

[15]In *Missionization and Hispanicization of Santo Tomas Apostol de Abiquiu, 1750–1770*, Gilberto Benito Córdova (1979) referred to the compilation of Spanish laws relating to the treatment of Indians in the New World. Córdova cited *reducción* laws relevant to the settlement of Northern New Mexico on pages 242–256. The four-volume *Recopilación* was originally published by Charles II in 1681. The Laws of Burgos were a forerunner of the *Recopilación*; they attempted to ensure Indian rights as the Indians became Hispanicized Christians. This process of transition from one culture to another involved the loss of a previous culture, not just the acquisition of another. Roots of the *genízaro* extend to the Old World, where late-16th-century Turks placed young Christian captives, known as *janizaries*, in Muslim families to convert the Christians and their allegiance.

[16]Although the pageant lapsed in 1913 for reasons that remain unclear, Anglos revived and revised what has become known today as the Santa Fe Fiesta.

[T]he New Mexicans conceived of two *Mexicanos*, one living in New Mexico and another below the border. Because both groups have comparable folk heritages, with similar folk songs, folk tales, foods, and customs, it is logical to include them under the same cultural category *"Mexicano"* when expressed in Spanish. But obviously the English term "Mexican" did not convey the same meaning to the New Mexicans. It became a purely national term, and because the informers were American citizens, they felt that the term did not accurately identify them. (p. 5)

With only 27 years of Mexican control (1821–1848) over the remote region, the area culture had little time to invest in a "Mexican" identity (Donato, 1999).

Political consciousness in the 1960s and 1970s challenged the distinction some Spanish-speaking Northern New Mexicans were trying to make about appearance, origin, and social class. Taking their cue from Blacks, Spanish-speaking political activists across the country adopted the term *Chicano*, once a pejorative term for low-class Mexicans (Acuña, 1988). In a poem entitled "Chicano," Rosa Elvira Alvarez (1971) emphasized the underprivileged status of the Chicano:

> "The word Chicano is a reproach
> An anguish with something of a hope ...
> It is a challenge, perhaps a banner
> The stubborn standard of a race ..." (p. 11).

For those Northern New Mexicans proud of their Mexican and Indian backgrounds, the political connotation of *Chicano* has come to represent their nativism, their resistance against injustices caused by the colonization of New Mexico, and their dedication to reclaiming communal land grants converted into national forest by the United States government (González, 1985). *La Raza* (The People) and *Paisanos* (Native Villagers) slogans rally protesters against Anglo domination in Northern New Mexico. Those identifying with their Meso-American roots and the struggle against Anglo oppression prefer *Chicano*; those identifying with their Spanish-speaking heritage accept the designation *Hispano* or *Hispanic*.[17]

---

[17]Adrian Herminio Bustamante (1982) surveyed 253 villagers in Pecos, Peñasco, Taos, Hernandez, and Abiquiu about ethnic self-identification. Of the nearly 40 different terms used, 50.6% related to Hispanic origin and 45.4% to Mexican ancestry or the Chicano movement (p. 174). Ethnic term preference of selected college students at the University of New Mexico showed only 4% identifying themselves as Spanish Americans, whereas 91% of Northern New Mexico Community College students self-identifed as Spanish American or Spanish (p. 178). Bustamante's study analyzed comparative data by residence (urban or rural) and age.

While militant groups sponsor political causes in the name of *chicanismo*, *hispanismo* dominates the titles of books and monographs and newspaper headlines in Northern New Mexico. Heightened ethnic awareness, combined with increased immigration from Spanish-speaking countries during the 1970s and 1980s, led to the emergence of a pan-Hispanic identity centered in a common language. Jerry Apodaca, former governor of New Mexico, began publishing the *Hispanic* magazine to promote pan-Hispanic unity regardless of nationality or background. The idea of "Hispanicness"—that Spanish-speaking Americans have a common goal in responding to problems of discrimination—initiated a debate about terminology between those who prefer to align their political community and class visions with Latin America and those who align themselves with Spain.

Cultural associations fuel the *Latino* versus *Hispanic* dispute. Those who defy their Spanish colonial heritage prefer *Latino* because it joins them to other Western Hemisphere speakers of Latin-based languages (Fox, 1996). Some refuse both terms because both terms deny Indian ancestry (Anzaldúa, 1999). Others dispute the labeling itself, and rather than romanticizing one culture over another, they celebrate their mixed ancestry: "It is in the richness of our *mestizaje* where our strengths lie" (Romero, 1992, p. 12). Taos artist Pola Lopez de Jaramillo commented on New Mexican identity politics in her painting *Who Wins This Game?* The painting depicts tic-tac-toe squares illustrating the ideology of each different label—Mexican American, Chicano, Spanish American, Latino, Mestizo, Hispano, Hispanic, Minority/other.

Most Hispanics in Northern New Mexico are *norteños*—northerners—who distinguish their cultural heritage from that of Mexicans who settled in the state (Bustamante, 1982). Norteños are not recent immigrants. They self-identify by family names that trace roots to Northern New Mexican villages, not to Europe or Mexico. A typical conversation between strangers from the region begins by placing each other according to their family and community affiliations.

In this book I use the ethnic label *Hispano* because it comes closest to defining Norteños by their regional homeland in Northern New Mexico and Southern Colorado. Their homeland's cultural landscape reflects adjustments to a natural environment over a long time (Carlson, 1990; Nostrand, 1992). Although critics of the homeland concept disagree with distinguishing Hispano culture as a subset of Mexican Americans or Chicanos in the U.S. Southwest, most acknowledge the utility of the term because the region has undergone a common "experience of conquest, subordination, penetration, widespread local displacement, and continuing pressure upon its integrity" (Meinig, 1984, cited in Van Ness, 1987, p. 3).

The distinct Spanish spoken in the region combines archaic 16th-century rural Castilian with Mexican Indian and Rio Grande Indian vocabulary, idiomatic expressions peculiar to the Spanish of Mexico, and countless language items from English, which the Spanish-speaking segment of the population has borrowed and adapted for everyday use (Cobos, 1983).[18] Decreed colonial settlement near pueblos exposed Indians to the Spanish way of life and resulted in a unique Norteño folk culture—a blend of Catholicism and Spanish material culture with Indian corn culture, ceremonials, craftsmanship, architectural design, dry farming, medicinal plants, and customs.

Not everyone who can claim *Hispano* identity will do so, or do so consistently:

[T]he answer to "What am I?" is always provisional and negotiable. There is no such thing as an *authentic* identity, ethnic or otherwise. There are only the identities that we make up, or that others make up and impose on us, and the one that sticks evolves in an ongoing process of assertion and reaction. Identities are subject to change and must be actively defended if they are to be preserved. (Fox, 1996, p. 16)

The assertion of identity begins with the reinterpretation of the past, which is a never-ending project. The promoters of a new identity want to be able to declare definitively, "We are what we are because we got this way, and these are the events that made us." Nothing about the past, however, is definitive. The past is multiple and various, so filled with events real and fictitious that they can be combined to tell many different stories, and all interpretations are subject to shifts as people begin asking new questions about the present. (Fox, 1996, p. 189)

---

[18]Rubén Cobos first became acquainted with New Mexico Spanish by listening to his classmates at the Menaul School in Albuquerque who came from the villages of Northern New Mexico. Neddy Vigil and Garland Bills, directors of the New Mexico and Colorado Spanish Survey project, are documenting the various Spanish dialects used in the Southwest while recording oral histories for the University of New Mexico's Center for Southwest Research. For more information about sociolinguistic studies of New Mexican and Southern Colorado Spanish, consult *Spanish and English of United States Hispanos: A Critical Annotated, Linguistic Bibliography,* edited by Richard Teschner, Garland Bills, and Jerry R. Craddock (1975), and *Guide to Reference Works for the Study of the Spanish Language and Literature and Spanish American Literature,* edited by Hensley C. Woodbridge (1997).

How schooling affects the evolving process of asserting, renegotiating, and defending an *Hispano* identity is this book's central concern. In the Norteño School District, narratives of remaining and becoming are shaped by public memories of documented political history mingled with more private memories. Each narrative develops different images about hard-won and inherited identities and how identity shifts.

2

Souls and Minds:
Norteño's Educational History

I came to Norteño to explore the linkage between school and community. Norteño High School's graduation day exemplifies this linkage in many ways, for it has become an integral part of the rhythm of community life that the whole community celebrates. Educational opportunity at the secondary and college levels came late to Northern New Mexico's villagers. Thus, high school graduation is a milestone. One community elder recalls:

> My father actually didn't have any formal schooling at all. Our school was very primitive, and the teachers themselves had very little training—probably a second or third grade education. But because they knew a little English, they were hired by the local board to be the instructors in that particular village. My mother also didn't have any schooling—maybe 1 year—because her parents used to say that the place of the lady was in the house. They were supposed to take care of the family, and the father had the duty of earning the living for the family (personal communication, October 27, 1992).

For many grandparents of the 1993 graduates, completing eighth grade warranted a graduation party. Nowadays, their grandchildren enjoy modern school facilities; teachers are bilingually certified; graduation occurs after twelfth grade; female valedictorians are not uncommon. Nearly 80% of the Norteño graduates, compared to only 14% 32 years ago, will receive postsecondary education in 4-year universities, community colleges, trade schools, or the military.[1] All of these facts represent a striking contrast to the schooling of the past.

---

[1]According to the 1992 *New Mexico School District and School Achievement Profiles*, the percentage of Norteño graduates pursuing postsecondary education   (*continued*)

As teenagers, parents of the current graduates faced different prospects: They had no guidance counselor to tell them how to apply to college or what to expect; there were few affirmative action policies for recruiting and supporting Hispanic students; their families needed them to earn extra income; males had the possibility of being drafted. Some parents struggled to be the first in their families to go to college; others hope that their children will have this distinction. Within the community, the socioeconomic gap has widened between the educated and undereducated, and between those earning income and those on welfare. With subsistence farming no longer a viable option, limited local employment opportunities make educational opportunities and the military attractive options for the young. Both options necessitate leaving the community, at least temporarily.

Weeks before graduation, invitations to parties are passed out in school and hand-delivered to homes. Conversations buzz about graduation: "How many invitations did you get? Which relatives are coming from out of town?" Houses are painted, bands booked, tents rented, and freezers filled in anticipation of hosting a party. Generosity and hospitality remain hallmarks of the region. Those attending the parties find their own way to acknowledge the achievements of the seniors, usually giving them an envelope containing money. A grandmother reminisces about graduates in her day receiving new socks and shaving kits.

No two invitations look alike; each carries a personalized message to family and friends. Cecilia's quotes Malcolm X: "Education is our passport to the future ... for tomorrow belongs to those who prepare for it today." Victor's sketch of Jesus and the Sacred Heart covers the front of his invitation: "Anything is Possible through God Who Strengthens Me." At the heart of most graduation messages lies the strong faith that exists in Northern New Mexico. Even the principal's yearbook message to the graduates reminds them of the presence of God in their lives: "You don't get to choose how you're going to die, or when; you can only decide how you're going to live, and having that choice, always put God first."

(*continued*) has increased 20% in the past 5 years. Henry Borgrink and his staff at the New Mexico Department of Education prepared this report to give a 3-year statistical comparison (1988–1991) of the 88 school districts in New Mexico. According to statistics provided in *Embudo: A Pilot Planning Project for the Embudo Watershed of New Mexico* (1962), only 14% of the 1960–61 Norteño graduates planned to enter college and 41% of those who entered college never graduated. This report was published by the Interagency Council for Area Development Planning and the New Mexico State Planning Office.

The Sunday before graduation, all 52 seniors, regardless of religious preference, participate in a baccalaureate ceremony at the Catholic Church. Graduation from the public high school itself used to take place there until local Protestants demanded the separation of church and state in the late 1940s. Before this dispute, the priest conducted mass in Latin and gave out the diplomas; not so today. Now the priest welcomes guests to the church and explains the rituals, inviting non-Catholics—Presbyterians, Mormons, Jehovah's Witnesses, Baptists—to say the Lord's Prayer in their own way. Such ecumenicalism was rare when the parents of today's seniors graduated from high school.

Lights dim as the seniors slowly file into the church, each carrying a lit candle and singing the refrain from one of their favorite religious songs, "Pass It On": "It only takes a spark to get a fire going ..." Some older women cover their heads as in the past, but younger people dress more casually, some even in jeans. High-top Nike tennis shoes, partially laced, show beneath a young altar boy's robe. The sermon is not delivered from the pulpit. Instead, the priest walks back and forth in front of the pews, addressing the seniors in a conversational tone. Father John holds up a silver dollar: "A silver dollar is the Church's gift to each of you. Where will it be in 20 years? Polished and on display for all to see, or tarnished and hidden in a drawer?" Father John's message reflects his community crusade to fight the excessive consumption of alcohol that tarnishes the lives of too many Norteños. He prays for the people these young adults can become.

The graduation ceremony at the high school takes place the following weekend in the new gymnasium, where basketball games draw big crowds during the winter months. At the ceremony, the strong Catholic faith of the local community clashes once again with the external edicts endorsing secular education. Aware of the 1992 Supreme Court decision outlawing prayer at commencement,[2] David—the salutatorian and one of nine seniors who attended the local parochial school before it closed for financial reasons in 1987—begins his speech: "No one will restrict me from thanking my Lord for his support." A round of applause erupts, including all the members of the board of education, who after long hours of debate reached a divided vote in favor of allowing prayer at commencement. For David and many others, no separation exists between church and school.

---

[2] In June 1992, the U.S. Supreme Court ruled 5 to 4 in *Lee v. Weisman* that "it was an unconstitutional government establishment of religion for a school district to invite clerics to deliver prayers at graduation" (Walsh, 1993, p. 1).

Covaledictorians Cecilia and Merlinda draw on symbols of popular culture for their speeches. Cecilia, once described in the student newspaper as "15% hippie," steps up to the podium with a peace symbol on her mortarboard and paraphrases "The Serenity Prayer": "God give me the serenity to accept things which cannot be changed, give me courage to change things which must be changed, and the wisdom to distinguish one from the other."

Cecilia encourages her classmates to aim high, quoting Jimi Hendrix's lyrics, "'Scuse me while I kiss the sky." In the fall she will attend Stanford. Merlinda reads from Dr. Seuss' *Oh, the Places You'll Go!* Merlinda will go to a New Mexico university. Like many of her classmates, she prefers to stay close to home.

While Cecilia and Merlinda focus on prospects of becoming, the charismatic guest speaker—a middle-aged, Hispano radio celebrity—addresses the tradition of remaining. His message about the past echoes the messages I heard throughout the year. In a dramatic gesture, he turns his back to the audience and faces the graduates to speak directly to them:

> I'm proud to be Hispanic. [applause] You're twice as valuable if you speak two languages. If you know your language, you have your culture no matter what your clothes look like. *Y si hablan español, los gringos no entienden. Pero los gringos no entienden nada.* [If you speak Spanish, the Anglos won't understand. But the Anglos don't understand anything anyway!] [laughter]

> As long as you have the love and support of your community, you have everything. What you have here is something kids who grow up in the city don't have.

> What is success? We always measure it by the wrong means. To me, success is helping someone, expecting nothing in return. I'm successful, not because of my car and house. I measure success on my own scale by making people laugh and be happy.

The guest expresses little serenity about change. He asks these graduates to have the courage and wisdom not to change.

His words reaffirm what other adults have told me about the changes going on in the community: the loss of language, culture, and intimacy. The parents of the seniors grew up in isolated villages; their children grow up with the outside world slipping readily into homes by satellite dish and cable television, both of which came to the valley in the past decade.[3] Parents reached school having spoken only Spanish at home; few of their children speak Spanish fluently.

The joke about the Anglos "not knowing anything anyway" discloses a sense of outrage many Hispano adults harbor. Their bad memories include reprimands for speaking Spanish in school and feeling that something about being Hispano must be wrong if they needed to change to succeed. As Hispanos experienced Anglo education and learned Anglo concepts of opportunity, success meant going away to become more educated and to make something of themselves. Financial constraints, inadequate academic preparation, hesitancy about English, and ambivalence about the nature and implications of new opportunities made the transition to the outside world difficult. Though these parents returned to live in Norteño, most must compete in the Anglo world, where they experience the rub between the cultures.

The ceremony ends with the seniors squirting each other with spray confetti—a sign of the times. As guests flow from party to party, heavy traffic fills the roads between the villages. At each home, the hosts put out a generous spread, so one has to pace oneself to eat with appetite throughout the afternoon. At one party, Reyes Pacheco, a middle-aged man, describes the dramatic changes in Norteño these past 40 years. The country lifestyle of his childhood meant chores before and after school. The alfalfa had to be irrigated, the hay baled and stacked, the cows milked and fed, the acequias cleaned. Weekends were spent hauling and splitting wood, the primary source of heat. Rabbit hunting or fishing with his father and brothers filled his free time. The land anchored, defined, and nourished his life.

Reyes recalls how participating in community events like *las matanzas* [communal hog butchering] and *paseando* [visiting] used to be favorite social activities. He remembers how "family blood was thicker then. Families were really tight, close-knit. We were always out doing things together." Nowadays, he laments, people do not visit each other as much. Fewer families farm, so children spend more time with peers than with relatives and neighbors. The resiliency, discipline, and motivation once learned from a rural lifestyle in a close-knit community must now be learned from other life experiences, including schooling.

Norteño's present school campus, with attractive buildings and modern facilities, in no way resembles the scattered buildings Reyes remem-

---

[3]Cable television started service to the Norteño area in 1990.

bers. Reyes first attended a one-room village school, before the school district was consolidated. An iron stove heated the adobe schoolhouse, and water was gathered from the ditch running through the village. There was no playground equipment. Later Reyes took the bus to the secondary school in Norteño, where being a Protestant sometimes got him into fistfights.

As Reyes describes his life, an intriguing story unfolds. I learn about the traditional agrarian lifestyle that once buffered Norteño families from the Anglo world. He speaks of geographical isolation, intercultural power struggles, sectarian education, and educational inequality, all of which have shaped the development of the villages and the development of the schools. Reyes' longitudinal perspective helps me recognize the significance of the educational changes that have taken place in Norteño and the context such changes provide for understanding today's educational debates. His historical perspective underscores the controversy about whether local schools should prepare children to leave Norteño or to resist assimilation, educational functions perceived as essentially contradictory.

A LEGACY TO RECKON WITH

The cultural and geographical characteristics of Northern New Mexican villages determined how schools were established in the region. Colonial policies, first of Spain, then of Mexico, and later of the United States, shaped the development of this remote area where three cultures eventually met—the Indians native to the region, the Spaniards from southern Europe by way of Mexico, and the Northern Europeans by way of the United States. Each colonial power had a different agenda for education. The power struggles that plagued the relationships between these cultural groups were played out in the educational history of Northern New Mexican villages (see Fig. 2.1).

Spanish Colonization (1598–1821)

Spanish settlements began as defensive outposts on the northeastern edge of New Spain's frontier [New Mexico] to prevent encroachments by rival colonial powers. The first Spanish colonists arrived in Northern New Mexico in 1598. The early colonial policy of Spain required every expedition of *conquistadores* to be accompanied by Franciscan priests, who were responsible for the missionization and hispanicization of the indigenous

No Public Schools; Private Schools & Tutors	First Public School Taxation Failed	Poor Public Schools	Presbyterian Mission School Opened in Norteño	Midwestern Nuns Opened Public Schools in Norteño	Secular Public Schooling Legal Dispute	Secular Norteño Public School District Created
1700s Norteño Settled in New Spain	1821 Mexican Independence	1848 American Occupation	1860s Protestant Missionaries Arrived	1926 Fourteen Years After Statehood	1949 Dixon Case	1950 Consolidation of Village Schools Begins

FIG. 2.1.   Historical bench marks affecting education in Norteño.

populations and the captive nomadic Indians placed as servants in settler households. The viceroy of New Spain instructed these priests to use education for political control of the Indians, through conversion, apprenticeship labor, and cultural instruction. Indians learned skills and trades needed for economic development and learned how to play musical instruments and read hymns needed for mass. The language of instruction was Latin, not Spanish. By the late 1700s, one third of New Mexico's population was *genízaro*—hispanicized and Christianized Indians.[4]

To satisfy the needs of the expanding Spanish colonial population and to encourage settlement of outlying areas as buffers against Comanche raids, the Spanish Crown established a system of land grants. Accordingly, Spanish settlers first came to live in the valley north of Norteño some time after 1700.[5] These original land grant owners abandoned their land, possibly because of hostile Indians, so that in 1796 new Spanish settlers took possession of the valley and requested permission to build towns (deBuys, 1985).

Spain's exclusionary mercantile policy closed the borders of the Province of New Mexico to foreign trade or exploration, thereby isolating the

---

[4]The ethnohistorical significance of the *genízaro* grew as Indians were uprooted and placed in Spanish families and female Indian servants bore children out of wedlock to Spanish householders. Albert H. Schroeder (1972) discussed this numerical increase in "Rio Grande Ethnohistory," as did Gilberto Benito Córdova (1979) in *Missionization and Hispanicization of Santo Tomas Apostol de Abiquiu, 1750–1770*. Bernardo Phillip Gallegos (1988) examined the relationship of schooling, religious hegemony, and social control in *Literacy, Schooling, and Society in Colonial New Mexico: 1692–1821*.

[5]According to Blanche Grant's May 1936 Works Progress Administration report about Norteño, this land grant is described in the private land claim No. 114. Works Progress Administration reports are available in the New Mexico State Archives.

Spanish colonial settlers. Only one trade route linked the northern colonial settlements to Mexico—the Camino Real, or King's Highway, which ran 1,500 miles from Chihuahua in the south to Santa Fe in the north. A section of the Camino Real known as the Summer Trail extended to Norteño, but trade caravans were few and far between. Spain's trade policy thus established the "separateness" of the people in Norteño:

> Isolated from each other as well as from the outside world, they were left to their own resources, scarcely touched by changes or new trends in Europe or New Spain. With no stimulus to change the only values and customs they knew, the colonists held to their traditional way. (Warren, 1987, p. 5)

Mexican Rule (1821–1848)

After New Spain broke away from the crumbling Spanish empire, independent nations formed throughout South and Central America. In 1821, Mexico declared its independence and its sovereignty over the northeastern frontiers that included New Mexico. The Mexican congress attempted to establish a state system of primary schools. In 1824 half of the tithes collected by the government were directed to a public school fund, and the first schools were opened in Santa Fe, Albuquerque, and Santa Cruz de la Cañada. These schools closed 10 years later when frontier colonists protested the collection of tithes. After the public school closure, New Mexicans returned to the educational system they had lived with under Spanish administration—private tutors and private schools for the children of wealthy families only.

During the Mexican colonial era (1821–1848), Father Martínez, an influential priest in Taos, campaigned for public education. Believing that literacy was the source of empowerment for the local population, he founded the first coeducational school in New Mexico at his home around 1826. He is credited with publishing *El Crepúsculo*, the state's first newspaper, to urge land reform, to fight against taxation by the Mexican government, and to promote public education. Ironically, his crusade against taxation contributed to the demise of public schools when the Mexican congress withdrew the civil obligation to pay tithes in 1833 and the school fund dwindled in the hands of the clergy (Sanchez, 1940/1967).[6]

---

[6]According to the Presbyterians, Father Martínez declared himself in favor of religious freedom and taught his people that the Bible was the Word of God and that eternal life came from faith, not penance and works. He either resigned from his post or was excommunicated in 1858. See Reverend David Reiter (1963), "Presbyterians at Work Long Before Organization of Synod."

Although the northern villages at first experienced little change under the Mexican government, real change was about to occur. When Mexican authorities failed to enforce the exclusionary trade policies that the Spanish colonial regime had imposed, Anglo trappers, traders, and prospectors began to arrive. The soon-to-be-famous wagon trail from Missouri to Santa Fe opened in 1821; once opened, the trail breached 2 centuries of isolation. At first, Anglo settlers trickled into the territory. By the turn of the 20th century, the trickle became a torrent, resulting in an Anglo majority in the state sometime after 1920. The Anglos lived mostly in the Rio Abajo region south of Santa Fe (González, 1967). In Northern New Mexico, Hispanos never have lost their majority status, because Hispano control of property, lack of industrialization, and limited economic development make the region unattractive to outsiders. According to New Mexico's 1990 census, 65% of the residents in Norteño's county are Hispanos (U.S. Department of Commerce, 1992a, p. 10).

United States Occupation (1848–1912)

At the close of the war with Mexico in 1848, the United States' occupation of New Mexico began with the fateful signing of the Treaty of Guadalupe Hidalgo. Growing villages like Norteño became focal points of cultural interaction as the U.S. Army established outposts nearby. General Stephen Kearny, an agent of the expanding United States, entered New Mexico with the spirit of a crusader carrying the banner of liberty to an oppressed people. The Kearny Code proclaimed universal literacy for prospective citizens: "Schools and means of education shall be forever encouraged in the Territory. One or more schools shall be established in each village as soon as practical, where the poor shall be educated free of all charge" (Moyers, 1941, p. 145).

Kearny's promise of free public education in the territory was not fulfilled. According to the 1850 census, of New Mexico's total population of 61,549, only 466 children were in parochial schools, none in public schools (Lavender, 1980). For 50 years, the U.S. Congress refused multiple appeals by territorial governors for federal support of a New Mexico school system:

> The United States government made its customary donation of school lands to New Mexico by the Organic Act of September 9, 1850. But these lands were unsurveyed and unsalable. They were not valuable because the good lands had practically all been granted to private parties before American occupation. The legislature repeatedly petitioned Congress for other

aid in the form of money grants or grants of land in other states for school purposes, but Congress took no action. (Moyers, 1941, p. 188)

Passage of the Fergusson Act in 1898 finally provided for the sale of public lands to support public schools in the Territory of New Mexico and promised more land grants upon admission into the union as a state.

Anglo authorities urged the territorial legislature to make provisions for public education, but the territorial government encountered tremendous antagonism to paying taxes to support common schools. As early as 1856, a school tax law for building schools was almost unanimously rejected in a referendum.[7] When school laws did pass, they received inadequate funds. Why such determined opposition to public education? Part of the answer is historical. Having revolted against direct taxation by Mexico earlier in the century, Hispanos continued to be reluctant taxpayers. They were particularly opposed to paying taxes to support a type of education that they feared would corrode traditional values. In 1889, the territory's Catholic hierarchy opposed the proposed state constitution because of a secular school provision:

> The Catholic leaders claimed that the governor and those advocating the establishment of public schools were attempting to exclude morality, to set up "Godless schools," that is, schools in which the religious element was left out. [Secular school advocates'] real aim was to de-Catholicise New Mexico. This would be accomplished by employing only Protestant teachers. They believed that "as is the teacher so is the school." (Moyers, 1941, pp. 337–338)

Until the 1890s, politicians in the Hispano-dominated territorial legislature successfully opposed public education and its presumed Americanizing effects, preferring instead schools taught in Spanish that transmitted Roman Catholic principles and educated boys and girls separately (Forrest, 1989; Weinberg, 1977). Many Hispano politicians opposed statehood because "it meant Anglo-American rule [from Washington], taxes, public schools, anti-Church policies, and the acquisition of their remaining lands" (Acuña, 1988, p. 75). While other territories hastened to become states, New Mexico remained a territory for 65

---

[7]The vote against local taxation for schools in the counties of Taos, Rio Arriba, Santa Ana, and Socorro was 5,016 to 37. See the Las Vegas *Daily Optic* 1893 series titled "Education in New Mexico" in the Frank Reeves Collection at the University of New Mexico's Center for Southwest Research.

years, partially by choice but also by exclusion. Distrust of New Mexico's essentially foreign culture and a strong Protestant bias against the territory's Catholic hierarchy obstructed New Mexico's statehood aspirations (Bustamante, 1982; Larson, 1971).

In spite of fear of Anglo domination and of Hispano children being educated away from the Catholic Church, Hispanos increasingly resented the second-class American citizenship that they had as residents of a territory. They eventually joined Anglos in championing statehood. Knowing that the provision for public education was a condition for admission into the union, territorial lawmakers finally passed bills in the 1890s that established a territorial board of education with a Catholic Hispano, Amado Chaves, appointed as the first territorial superintendent of public instruction. The board created a uniform system of textbooks, authorized local boards to levy school taxes and to issue bonds for the erection of schoolhouses, opened public secondary schools, made school attendance compulsory, and mandated English as the language of instruction in schools. Enforcement of this original English-only law was lax, but the spirit of the law led to legislative debates about language that continue today (Leibowitz, 1985).

In 1909, as part of the campaign for statehood, the territorial government published its first uniform course of study—*The Manual of the Common School Course of Study for the Public Schools of New Mexico*:

Fifty-eight pages of "Memory Gems" were included, and classified by years, for pupils to commit to memory. All of these selections were poetry except one—Lincoln's "Gettysburg Address." Some of these "gems" were: "Harvest Song," "The Rainbow Fairies," "What the Winds Bring," "New Year Song," "Wynken, Blynken and Nod," "A Visit from St. Nicholas"....

There were sixty-four "Flag Days" to be observed in the schools by display of the United States flag and appropriate programs. Among these days to be observed were Perry's Victory on Lake Erie, the First Continental Congress, Louisa M. Alcott, Assistance from France Promised, Shakespeare, Ticonderoga Taken, and New Mexico day. A notable omission was Coronado Day.... No Spanish hero except Columbus was honored by a "Flag Day." (Moyers, 1941, pp. 329–330)

Given nationalist sentiments, the authors of the curriculum modeled the New Mexican courses on American common schools, disregarding the history and culture of the Hispano children. Critics of the curriculum argued that these educational practices reflecting American cultural standards and traditions failed to help most Hispanos improve their everyday conditions.

At the same time, the territorial legislature also established six 4-year colleges that drew students from across the territory and from Arizona, Texas, Colorado, and Mexico. Funding for Hispano village schools suffered as a consequence of diverting scarce territorial funds from common schools to higher education. Moreover, poverty, inadequate rural elementary school facilities, lack of public high schools in Northern New Mexico counties, and discrimination excluded almost all but the wealthiest Hispanos from higher education.

Finally, with yet another fateful stroke of a pen, the tide of Americanization overwhelmed the last resistance. In 1912, the U.S. government declared New Mexico a state. The public educational system promised since the Treaty of Guadalupe Hidalgo became a reality, and both the Catholic Church and Protestant groups responded to the need for educators in Northern New Mexico. The rhyme of American poems like "Wynken, Blynken and Nod" and biblical verses were to change the rhythm of a lifestyle set by centuries of Hispano tradition.

THE RISE OF SECTARIAN SCHOOLS: RELIGION AND CULTURE

Defiende nuestra cultura y los valores de nuestra ser
(Defend our culture and the values of our being)
              —*"Madre Morena,"* A Catholic hymn

Ironically, the story of Norteño's public school district begins with religious rivalry. When New Mexico became a U.S. territory, the Catholic hierarchy deemed that public schools were Protestant places. Reflecting Catholic opposition to the incursion of Protestant values, a proclamation was issued by Bishop Lamy to start Catholic-run schools. The Sisters of Loretto, the first teaching order of nuns, came by wagon train from the Midwest in 1852 to start the first Catholic school in New Mexico, for girls. Somewhat later, the order of Christian Brothers came to teach boys (Atkins, 1982; "Barring of Nuns Upheld," 1951).

New Mexico's majority population being Catholic, a bill won passage in 1878 to create county school systems that incorporated both religious and nonsectarian schools. "The act ... permitted the [Association of Jesuit Fathers] to establish and conduct educational institutions, to own real property, and to be exempt from taxation" (Atkins, 1982, p. 352). Despite federal separation of church and state, this territorial bill joined them, thereby setting the pattern for church–government cooperation for the next 70 years. In exchange for the Catholic Church's almost unconditional financial and political support of the territorial government, the state granted the Catholic Church a monopoly over education. Lamy, appointed archbishop in 1875, directed the Jesuits to establish schools, colleges, and other institutions wherever possible in the state (Acuña, 1988).

Jesuit dominance met Protestant opposition. At the heart of this rivalry for school control were the souls of children. Anglo Protestants saw New Mexico as a spiritual wilderness: "Fear of barbarism, and of a generation growing up on the frontier with no civilizing influence, compelled most of the major denominations to organize and fund missionary enterprises" (Atkins, 1982, p. 73). Intense suspicion of Catholics motivated Protestant missionaries to push for control of the educational system by English-speaking "secularists," knowing this meant schools to which they would have access.

Because Catholic priests strictly forbade the common people to possess Bibles, Protestant missionaries seized the opportunity to evangelize among people they labeled "the exceptional populations of the Southwest" (Free Schools Committee). Striking directly at Catholic prohibitions, they distributed Bibles written in Spanish to the villagers. To their disappointment, the missionaries discovered that few villagers could read. Presbyterians concluded that their major missionary emphasis should be educational rather than pastoral. In 1867, Reverend D. F. McFarland wrote a letter to the Female Bible Society in Auburn, New York:

> In behalf of Christ's suffering cause and the dying souls of New Mexico, accept my warmest and most sincere thanks for your great interest and proposed aid to spread the Bible, God's own instrumentality for the conversion of sinful men in these morally dark and destitute regions. After full consultation with leading men who have been here for many years, I have reached the conclusion that an appropriation to employ [Christian ladies] to teach [free schools] will affect more the evangelization of the Spanish population than direct attempts to introduce the Scriptures among the people generally. (Barber & Agnew, 1981, p. 12)

Using preaching and teaching as pivotal weapons in the conversion arsenal, Protestants started mission schools. The first decade of Presbyterian missionary work concentrated on three areas: Santa Fe (1866), Las Vegas (1869), and Taos (1872). The height of Presbyterian activity in the northern part of the state lasted from the 1880s to about

1915 (see Fig. 2.2).[8] Presbyterian mission schools, known as *plaza* grade schools, opened in Hispano villages to provide kindergartens and elementary education. Approximately 80% of the plaza grade school teachers were single, Anglo women in their 20s, most of whom came from the Midwest or Pennsylvania and spoke no Spanish on arrival in the villages. The Women's Board of Home Missions in New York expected its missionaries to teach the Bible, the English language, and American culture, always the American culture. Clearly, in the missionaries' view, the prevailing folk culture in this mission territory was alien, non-American, and fair game for undoing. The mission schools used an American common school curriculum to expose Hispanos to the civic ideals of mainstream American society and to aspects of American culture, such as clothing, standards of hygiene, and technology. The Protestant schools combined a program of religious instruction and practical training—scientific farming methods, health care and nursing, Spanish furniture making, and weaving.

Presbyterians considered their day and boarding schools the "opening wedge" for moral inculcation in their mission fields. Pupils who wanted a secondary education went off to the Presbyterian boarding schools in Santa Fe and Albuquerque:

> The boarding-school has been an Americanizing agency as well as a Christianizing power in New Mexico. The location of the schools has brought the isolated boy and girl into contact with modern civilization. English is acquired much more rapidly than in a day-school; the whole system is more intensive. (Meeker, 1917, p. 4)[9]

---

[8]Negotiations of the Permanent International Council on Spanish-Speaking Work in the Southwest resulted in an ecumenical agreement in 1913, whereby Methodists agreed to focus more on the southern part of the state. See Randi Jones Walker (1991), *Protestantism in the Sangre de Cristos 1850–1920.*

[9]The Matilda Allison School, founded in 1867, combined with the Mary James School (1908–1913). The Allison-James school in Santa Fe was originally only for girls through 12th grade and provided elementary education teacher certification courses. Later it became a coed junior high school, which closed in 1959. From 1881 to 1890, the John Menaul School served as a boarding school for Indian students. In 1895, it reopened as a school for Spanish-Speaking boys, becoming a coed high school in 1934. Today Menaul teaches day students and boarding students, grades 6 to 12, in the Presbyterian's only remaining postelementary school located in Albuquerque. For more information about the Presbyterian mission schools in New Mexico and Colorado, see Ruth K. Barber and Edith J. Agnew (1981), *Sowers Went Forth*; Mark T. Banker (1993), *Presbyterian Missions and Cultural Interaction in the Far Southwest*; R. Douglas Brackenridge and Francisco García-Treto (1974), *Iglesia Presbiteriana: A History of Presbyterians and Mexican Americans in the Southwest.*

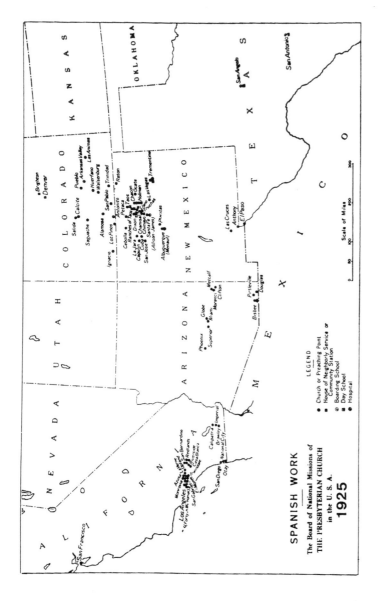

FIG. 2.2.   Spanish missions of the Presbyterian Church—1925. From *Iglesia Presbyteriana: A History of Presbyterians and Mexican Americans in the Southwest* (p. 154), by R. D. Brackenridge and F. García-Treto, 1974, San Antonio, TX: Trinity University Press. Copyright © 1974 by the Records of the Board of National Mission, Presbyterian Church in the U.S.A.; Presbyterian Historical Society, Philadelphia, PA. Reprinted with permission.

In the northern counties of Taos and Rio Arriba, poverty kept the few public schools poorly staffed and open for only 1 to 3 months a year. Hispanos who could not afford Catholic boarding schools took advantage of inexpensive, Anglo-run mission schools that were staffed for 9 months:

> Impoverished parents drove [their wagons] a hundred miles with their children, and mothers moved into town for the winter to send their children to these Protestant schools despite dire warnings by priests and the missions' package deal of Anglo skills wrapped in Anglo culture. (Deutsch, 1987, p. 27)

The Presbyterians successfully competed with the more expensive Catholic schools by opening mission schools in communities that could not collect enough taxes to qualify for matching state aid for education, and by charging minimal tuition fees, payable in kind. Between 1878 and 1891, the number of plaza grade schools grew from 6 to 29, including 1 in Norteño (1888–1909).[10]

Norteño's first mission teacher arrived in the autumn, after a 5-day trip from the East, to find herself in the Rockies among a people foreign in language, customs, race, and religion. An adobe structure, 13 by 15 feet, served as the first school until a chapel-school was built. People looked upon the young Anglo woman with suspicion and distrust, and the priest instructed them to avoid her. Throughout her time there, Norteño's teacher wrote about her mission school in the *Home Mission Monthly*:

> 1889—We labor under many difficulties here.... Many of our scholars do not enter school until about the middle of November or in December, the large boys being needed at their homes to watch their flocks and herds....
>
> All my scholars come from Catholic homes, with the exception of nine, whose parents are mostly Protestants. I am the only American here.
>
> 1894—The first year in the new [school] building proved very successful. The number of pupils enrolled was eighty-seven, of whom forty were between the ages of fifteen and twenty-four.
>
> The attendance on Song Service was remarkable, almost all the pupils were present with their parents or some of their friends, although some of the parents would not attend any of the other services. Our usual

---

[10]Depending on the source of information one looks at in the Menaul Historical Library in Albuquerque and New Mexico State Library in Santa Fe, the opening dates differ for Norteño's Presbyterian mission school. Some claim 1885; others 1886, 1887, 1888, or 1895. In 1950, a Presbyterian church was finally built in Norteño.

programme for this service was Scripture verses recited by the pupils in English and Spanish, two or three short prayers, and the singing of Gospel hymns in both the languages. The service seemed to be enjoyed by all and we trust that some good seed may have been sown for the Master.

Quite a number of families moved from other places into Norteño, that their children might attend the mission school.

1895—I made about fifty calls before school opened. I found the people very busy with their harvest, but kind and pleasant. Very many of the calls were made by the side of a threshing floor where the family were at work, or near the river bank where the women were busy washing or drying wheat.

1897—When I first came here nearly all the families had mud floors, which served for a table in the daytime and a bedstead at night. Now, in many of those houses we find board floors, bedstead, table, chairs, sewing machines and cooking stoves. The women can rest better and feel more at home when sitting on the floor, and in my room they will sometimes push aside the chair and sit down on the floor—they say, "to rest." A greater desire for education is also manifested. In my first school here I had about ten girls enrolled. Last year I had thirty-six girls … varying in ages from six years old to thirty years. The first year I came the people said, "Girls do not need to know how to read and write." Now they think differently about the matter and send their girls to school.

1901—I am glad to report that the saloon, quite near our Mission school, is closed … I was not in favor of saloons and taught temperance in the school.

1903—The Mission school was opened in October, 1888, with seven Mexican pupils. Four desks and a small table constituted our school furniture, but before Christmas, other desks, a globe, maps, Gospel song books and presents for a Christmas tree gladdened the hearts of both pupils and teacher. Our little adobe room was crowded to its utmost capacity to find space for the pupils who wished to enter the school.

It is now fifteen years since our little Mission school was opened, and we have enrolled about four hundred and fifty different pupils, ranging in age from five to thirty-five years. Many of these pupils never heard the Gospel story, nor came in contact with a Protestant teacher before entering my school. Now some of them are among our most consecrated workers, carrying the Gospel message to their own people in other parts of New Mexico. Many of my pupils are Roman Catholics, and about twenty families of the Penitentes were represented in school last year. Some of the pupils walk nearly five miles every day to attend.

1905—We had over a hundred small flags with which to decorate, and the pupils were very much pleased to wear the little flag on Norteño's first Fourth of July celebration. Besides the pupils' recitations, we had three good Spanish speakers from the patrons of the school, so that all could understand why we celebrated the Fourth of July. There were some very old people here, great-grandparents, who attended for the first time a meeting of the kind, and also listened to the recitations in English and Spanish of their grandchildren. It was the first Fourth of July celebration ever held in any of the plazas around.[11]

When the missionary teacher retired in 1909, the school was transferred to a neighboring village and then closed in 1919. Thereafter, some local children rode the train, affectionately known as the "Chili Line," south along the Rio Grande to Protestant boarding schools in relatively nearby Española and Santa Fe, and in the more distant Albuquerque. School choice created a religious rift in Norteño that divided families and villagers for decades. Priests denounced those who patronized mission schools, excommunicating some and threatening not to baptize the children or bury the dead of those who chose a Protestant education (Atkins, 1982; Unser, 1995). Hispanos who went off to boarding schools returned home more Americanized than their neighbors. Some who attended mission schools converted and took on temperance values. Some chose to teach or preach the Protestant doctrine in Northern New Mexico, and others pursued different careers elsewhere. Female literacy increased significantly.

Over the years, Presbyterians closed their plaza grade schools when adequate public schools opened. They devoted their support to expanding community services such as educational counseling, recreation programs, and adult activities. By 1949, only eight Presbyterian day schools and two Presbyterian boarding schools for Spanish-speaking children existed—Menaul in Albuquerque for boys and Allison-James in Santa Fe for girls. Today, only three Presbyterian schools remain: Menaul, now a coeducational boarding school for grades 6 to 12; an elementary school in Chimayó, and a day care school in Truchas.

---

[11]These excerpts are from the following issues of the Presbyterians' *Home Mission Monthly* (New York: Woman's Executive Committee of Home Missions of the Presbyterian Church): November 1889 to October 1890 (Vol. 4, p. 59); November 1894 to October 1895 (Vol. 9, p. 10); November 1895 to October 1896 (Vol. 10, p. 74); November 1897 to October 1898 (Vol. 12, p. 15); November 1901 to October 1902 (Vol. 16, p. 16); November 1903 to October 1904 (Vol. 18, p. 15); November 1905 to October 1906 (Vol. 20, p. 13).

Although the Presbyterian home-mission system put into motion a wave of change in the cultural landscape of Norteño, the missionaries themselves nevertheless remained on the fringes of Hispano culture. The community functions of the Catholic Church continued to sustain village life in Norteño. While plaza grade schools and a few experimental schools, like the Nambé Community School,[12] came and went, the Catholics made progress with their schools. Catholics not only actively established parochial schools, but also took over the operation of public schools in rural areas with Spanish-speaking students and in other areas where there were weak or no public schools, almost impassable roads, primitive school buildings, unattractive living conditions, and low salaries. The 1878 act that incorporated religious schools in county school systems helped Catholics regain control of public schools in Northern New Mexico. Catholics recruited priests and nuns as administrators and teachers and elected clergy to public school boards. The wall between church and state remained penetrable until it was reinforced by the New Mexico Supreme Court's 1949 ruling on the Dixon Case, a Protestant legal challenge to keep religion out of public schools.

THE DIXON CASE: A PROTESTANT SECULAR CHALLENGE TO CATHOLIC PUBLIC SCHOOLS

The story of Norteño's Catholic public education began when Father Peter Kuppers of Dixon, a Northern New Mexico village, challenged Pope Pius XI's request for American nuns to choose a mission in China instead of a school for Spanish-speaking children in Dixon. Father Kuppers won his case, and the Catholic Church sent four Dominican Sisters from Grand Rapids, Michigan, to work in Dixon's St. Joseph School, started by Father Kuppers in 1923 and operated with state funds. Norteño leaders eventually discovered that elsewhere in the state, public funds maintained schools where Catholic Sisters and Brothers taught. Why not for their children? they asked. An affirmative answer soon was forthcoming.

---

[12]I discuss the debates about the Nambé Community School (1937–1942) in chapter 3. It was a school–community development project that attempted to change the common school's role of "culture imposer" to the role of "culture stimulator." The community school had two objectives: to modify the curriculum to eliminate irrelevancy and conflict, and to make school the focal point of community development. See Lloyd Tireman and Mary Watson (1943), *La Comunidad: Report of the Nambé Community School*; Thomas Carter (1970), *Mexican Americans in School: A History of Educational Neglect*; David Bachelor (1990), *Educational Reform in New Mexico: Tireman, San José, and Nambé*.

In 1926, the county board of education gave Dominican Sisters the authority to run a public school in Norteño. The county school board agreed to pay teacher salaries but required the village to provide adequate facilities. Accordingly, the Sisters set up the school and convent largely from the community's Catholic parish resources; household items, school supplies, and gifts of money were sent from Michigan convents.[13] According to an account of the Grand Rapids Dominicans (Schwind, 1991, pp. 118, 142):

> [The school] opened with ninety-three pupils the first day of school. By the end of the year, there were that many in the primary room, 215 in the whole school.... The school was accredited as a two-year high school in 1928, and in 1930 as a fully accredited high school. In 1931 a new high school building was begun ... In 1934–1935 the congregation bought [Indian land] for approximately $15,000 to build a high school in [Norteño].

For almost 25 years, the Dominican Sisters taught and expanded the public school, grades K to 12; one of the Sisters even became the superintendent of the Norteño School District. The only way for children in surrounding villages to get a high school diploma without going away to a boarding school was to attend the secondary school in Norteño. Children walked or came on horseback to school; some students stayed with nearby relatives. A few families rented a place in Norteño for the winter so their children could go to school.

One Sister recalled her years teaching in Northern New Mexico, when all nuns wore habits and the job of teaching involved anything and everything:

> The communities were very simple. They depended on the Sisters. The school was everything in a community: the gathering place, the social center. After school, the Sisters would go out and take care of the sick, cases of impetigo or whatever. There was no medical attention in that area. We distributed clothing sent from Michigan. We taught home economics to the women. It was real missionary work. ("Nuns Were Pioneers," 1974)

Looking back on the impact of the nuns coming to Norteño, one current educator comments:

> The nuns were the first teachers we had with a college education. They were Anglo, so that helped with learning English, and bringing in outside

---

[13]In 1975, the archbishop of Santa Fe published *50 Years of Love, Praise and Service* in honor of the Grand Rapids Dominican Sisters who served Northern New Mexico from 1925 to 1975.

ideas and outside help. They taught the young generation what the outside world had to offer.

The nuns insisted that the children speak only English in school. One Norteño couple remembers how they struggled with learning catechism, taught in English from 8:30 to 9:00 every school morning. The wife managed because she was a good memorizer. She did not understand what she was learning, but she could repeat it word for word. Change was coming in through the back door of the church.

Even though the priests and nuns came from outside the region, their primary charge was to make good Catholics, not Americans, of Norteños. Crucifixes hung on the classroom walls, and religious training was part of the curriculum. Seniors enrolled in a special Catholic sociology class, and the catechism class was listed on report cards as "etiquette." The priest held confessions in the library. Children would dress up as saints on All Saints' Day (November 1), not as witches and goblins on Halloween.

Some Norteño Protestants who attended public schools run by Catholics recollect the problems they faced on account of their religious beliefs:

Mass was held every morning before school started, so even in the winter, we Protestants had to stand outside until it was over.

The priest told the Catholic children not to associate with us. He would say, "The Catholic Church is the only Church, and you commit a mortal sin if you go into any other church." I used to have to cut across some fields on my way to school to avoid getting beaten up.

One day my father discovered the catechism book I had been given in school. He was angry and told me, a fourth grader, to give it back to the nun. I was so terrified to confront the teacher that I burnt the book and lived in fear of being caught!

Religious tensions escalated in Northern New Mexico in the 1940s, as Protestants objected to nuns and priests being paid from public funds, wearing robes and habits when teaching public schools, and forcing religious instruction on all pupils. Protesters in Dixon, a village of some 1,200—mostly Hispanos, about half of whom were Protestants of various persuasions—complained:

The catholic prayer of devotion, Hail Mary, was recited by all students four times a day. Bingo was played in the school during [school] hours to raise money for the Catholic Church. Students were urged to go to confessional and were deprived of privileges if they refused; great advantages were given to pupils who memorized the Catholic catechism. (Earle, 1949, p. 2)

The protesters, concluding that a court case would be their only hope for remedying the situation, banded together. Fearing that their objections would not get a fair hearing at the state level, the Free Schools Committee published *Appeal for Free Schools*, a pamphlet to raise financial support to carry their fight for secular schools to the United States Supreme Court. The pamphlet linked what was happening in a small New Mexican village to a nationwide problem:

> The New Mexico situation is a part of a nation-wide problem facing all who are interested in maintaining the separation of church and state. The New Jersey school bus decision, the North College Hill problem, the McCollum case, the North Dakota vote against garbed nuns, the Eleanor Roosevelt–Cardinal Spellman controversy, are recent incidents along the same line in other parts of the country. The Organization of Protestants and Other Americans United for Separation of Church and State hopes to meet this issue squarely and on a nation-wide scale. (Free Schools Committee)

Historian Louis Avant estimated that in 1940, one out of every 10 New Mexico students was enrolled in a Catholic-run school ("Nuns Were Pioneers," 1974). By 1941, Catholics operated 31 public schools that obtained money from state and county officials (Moyers, 1941). The post–World War II association of Catholicism with Fascist Italy fueled the Catholic–Protestant debate over control of the schools in Northern New Mexico. The heat of the legal battle in Dixon spilled over into other villages. In Norteño, impassioned Protestants tried to close the Catholic-run school themselves by boarding it up. One Catholic woman describes her terror when prospects for maintaining the Catholic presence in her elementary school were dim:

> We envisioned some tall, mean, monstrous men coming into our school and taking the crucifix down from the walls. I remember we were ready to hide our catechism books. We lived in fear for quite some time, realizing that our education system would change, and we didn't know what harm would come to all of us.

> For many years, the majority of Protestants hated Catholics and vice versa. I remember even in later years when we had P.T.A. meetings in school and the officers asked our parish priest to open the meeting with prayer. A handful of people objected—especially to the sign of the cross.

The Catholic–Protestant controversy over the control of public schools, which had started in the 1870s, finally came to a head. In an effort to terminate the church–state cooperation established nearly 70 years earlier, the Free Schools Committee filed their case. On March 10, 1948, a front-page headline of *The Santa Fe New Mexican* read: "Suit Demands Removal of Nuns from Public-School Positions." At the time of the *Zellers v. Huff* case, commonly known as "The Dixon Case," county school boards and superintendents of 10 Northern New Mexico counties had given the Catholic Church the authority to run local public schools, including the school in Norteño.[14] In addition to Catholic nuns, the list of 235 defendants included members of the state board of education, the archdiocese of New Mexico, and local and county school boards.

The district court determined that 12 of the northern village schools were really Catholic parochial schools being subsidized in part by funds raised through state taxation. Norteño was 1 of the 12. The ruling banned 143 nuns and priests from ever again teaching in New Mexico public schools; it removed public schools from Catholic buildings, ended free bus transportation for parochial school pupils, prohibited issuing free textbooks to parochial schools, barred teaching sectarian doctrines and displaying sectarian symbols in public schools, and prohibited the payment of public tax funds to teachers in parochial schools ("Cleric Garb Banned," 1951; Earle, 1949; *Zellers v. Huff*, 1951).

Although the judgment was a victory for the Free Schools Committee in Dixon, its members appealed to the New Mexico Supreme Court in 1949 to close two loopholes. New Mexico's attorney general, Joseph Martínez, had ruled that the district court decree did not prevent other members of Catholic orders from taking the places of those banned. He also allowed boards of education to supply parochial school pupils with free religious books published by the state. A favorable decision from the New Mexico Supreme Court ultimately banned clerics who remained in public schools from wearing religious garb and prohibited the state from publishing faith readers for Catholic schools. As late as 1953, a law added

---

[14]The Dixon Case is named after the community that initiated legal action in 1947. At the time, an equal number of Catholics and Protestants lived in Dixon. However, the Catholic Church provided the teachers in the public schools. The New Mexico State Archives in Santa Fe has a Robert Jones Collection of newspaper clippings and pamphlets on the Dixon Case. The collection documents the case primarily from the Protestant perspective in the suit. A copy of the state supreme court ruling on *Zellers v. Huff* (1951) is available in the New Mexico Collection of the state library.

a provision to the state constitution to ensure that public schools would be free from sectarian control.

Catholic leaders bitterly denounced these rulings. Some interpreted them as no less than a Protestant effort to cripple the Roman Catholic Church. Looking back on how the Dixon Case affected Norteño, a Catholic woman laments the loss of religious instruction in the schools:

> The Dixon Case changed our community tremendously. Before there was much more respect for moral values and human dignity. As God has been taken out of school, we see the results. We realize that education in any aspect is good, but faith values are important to hold on to. The Dixon Case is like a bad dream waking up to reality and seeing that faith is not taken away so easily. Catholic faith lives in the hearts and minds of people. As my dad used to say, "What you are and what you know no one can take away from you."

The Dixon Case ruling marked the start of widespread Catholic parochial education—now labeled as such—in the state. In Norteño, the priest was able to convince the banned Dominican Sisters to return from Grand Rapids in 1950 to reorganize a local K to 6 parochial school with 137 students (Wiley, 1952).[15] When they did, school choice—Catholic or public—remained available for 37 years until dwindling finances forced the parochial school to close in 1987.

Up to 1950, two separate public school systems operated in the area: the K to 12 independent public school district run by the Catholic Church in Norteño and the elementary schools in the outlying villages run by the county school system. After the Dixon Case ruling, when the county board of education proposed to send Norteño's children to a school some 30 miles away, Norteños objected. They proposed that Norteño's school district of 483 pupils be consolidated with 12 outlying village schools that had a total of 658 pupils (Committee for Consolidation, 1950). With temporary buildings and but a few lay teachers, a secular public school district opened in Norteño in 1950, beginning the slow process of consolidation.

The 12 outlying village schools that became part of the Norteño School District had suffered from neglect by the county. The Committee for Consolidation (1950) reported on the conditions of the schoolhouses,

---

[15]Information about private and parochial school enrollment is published in state educational reports. Norteño's K to 6 parochial school information first appeared in the 1950–1951 report by the state superintendent.

the smallest accommodating 19 pupils and the largest 135 pupils. In 10 of the schools, teachers worked in dilapidated rooms with poor sanitation, lighting, and ventilation. Water came by bucket from nearby wells or acequias, wood-fired stoves presented a fire hazard, classrooms were overcrowded, and little playground equipment existed.

Before departing in 1950, the Sister who was superintendent recommended that the high school principal, a local with a graduate degree, be appointed superintendent of the consolidated, secular school district. Raised a Catholic and educated at the Menaul boarding school, the local superintendent seemed a good choice to handle the volatile situation, but the transition period was difficult for him. The Presbyterians wanted to make sure he did not allow teachers to promote religion in any way. The Catholics politicized the school by trying to control employment opportunities.

The local superintendent began the process of consolidation—convincing villages to close their schools, raising funds to expand Norteño's facilities, and arranging to bus students—that took over 20 years. Working out of his house, he scrounged for teaching space and materials. The school district used three buildings on both sides of the highway to hold classes, while he negotiated to buy one from the archdiocese and to build another. The 1st year there were no buses. The children came from the villages the best way they could. Some walked, some came on horseback, and a few rode bicycles. The protracted process reflected the fiscal realities of Norteño and the tenacity of some villages to hold on to their own schools. The village that had competed with Norteño to be the site of the consolidated school district was the last to close its school, and that was in 1972.

The departure of the nuns eventually changed the composition of the faculty of Norteño schools from an Anglo majority to an Hispano majority. Consolidation increased Norteño's teaching staff from 19 in 1949 to 43 in 1950. Starting with only 16 out of 43 teachers holding college degrees, the superintendent still faced some local disapproval for using his New Mexico Highlands University contacts to bring in college graduates rather than hiring locals to teach. By 1955, 35 out of 44 teachers had degrees.[16]

From an administrative perspective, consolidation led to a more comprehensive school program, including better facilities, equipment, instructional materials, and staff development. From a social perspective,

---

[16]Information about teaching positions and training is published in state educational reports. From 1950 to 1955, the number of teachers holding a bachelor's degree increased from 15 to 29; the number of master's degrees increased from 1 to 6 (Lusk, 1956; Rose, 1950; Wiley, 1952).

consolidation changed the dynamics of the outlying villages. Some view consolidation as "bringing the villages out of the dark ages"; some regret the loss of village control over raising their children; some hate losing their village school as the center of their social life. One middle-aged man looks back on consolidation:

> When we came to the school in Norteño, that was our first encounter with students from other communities. We found that there was a lot of conflict, especially with the boys. A lot of physical fights and arguments took place, because the sports rivalries of the individual village elementary schools spilled over into the new school.
>
> The friendships among the kids changed for sure—right away. You started meeting other students from other communities. So you went home in the evenings, did the chores, and didn't associate with the kids who were neighbors. You had friends in different places. I think that expanded us to some extent, but broke the friendships with the community, with the other students our age.

Consolidation expanded the boundaries of village life, thereby changing patterns of social mingling.

Throughout this chapter, I have highlighted major historical events that affected the education of Norteños. Several important factors—colonization, resistance, coming out of isolation, Americanization, and secularization—create the social and political context for today's debates about education in Norteño. The isolation of the villages from the 1700s to 1950 kept away outside world influences for a long time, so the pace of change was slow until this past generation. Writing over 35 years ago, anthropologist Florence Kluckhohn said, "In the Spanish-American villages [such as Norteño] there was neither the need nor the opportunity for putting the melting pot on to boil" (Kluckhohn & Strodtbeck, 1961, p. 247). Now some adults worry about how to put a lid on the melting pot that is boiling over.

Problems with the quality and availability of education plagued remote Norteño for over 150 years. Education eventually brought the world to Norteño, and the dependence on sectarian schools brought Anglos to the area to teach and preach. New religious sects proselytized and exposed young people to new ways of looking at the world and their place in it. Missionaries precipitated community splits that contributed to the controversy between Protestants and Catholics over control of the schools. Education divided families into those who stayed home and those who left Norteño to acquire it, and into those who remained Catholic and those who converted. After the Dixon Case ruling, the need to secularize the schools marked an educational turning point in Northern New Mexican villages.

The empty parochial school building vividly reminds us that wherever located, schools are cultural battlegrounds. That they remain cultural battlegrounds should surprise no one. In response to the decades-long push to Americanize Norteño youth, the Norteño School District now faces pressure from insiders to bring back discarded traditions and to reclaim a language that was almost wiped out by the state legislature's vacillating policies on the language of instruction.

3

People Without a Language:
Language Without a People

In the beginning was the Word. And the Word was made flesh. It was so in the beginning and it is so today. The language, the Word, carries within it the history, the culture, the traditions, the very life of a people, the flesh. Language is people. We cannot even conceive of a people without a language, or a language without a people. The two are one and the same. To know one is to know the other.... As his language fades, the Hispano's identity with a history, with a tradition, with a culture, becomes more nebulous with each passing day.

—Ulibarri (1973, p. 1)

What will be the fate of Northern New Mexican Spanish? At the 1992 Wildflower Festival in Las Vegas, New Mexico, Nasario García of New Mexico Highlands University predicted it will be dead in 30 years: "The tenacity of Northern New Mexican Spanish since the 16th century makes its imminent loss so tragic. We've lost many of the old words for lack of use." No one disputes the continuing decline in traditional New Mexican Spanish-language use and facility, but blame for the loss of language goes around and comes around. Students and teachers blame the parents for not reinforcing Spanish at home; parents first blame their own teachers for punishing them for speaking Spanish, and then their children's teachers for not instilling the language in the young; former teachers blame the state for forcing them to comply with the English-only law; and, finally, the state department of education blames current teachers for not immersing students in Spanish.

But Nasario García's concerns go beyond language: "We're not raising culturally aware children. They're cultural orphans. The TVs and VCRs have taken the place of *cuentos*—the stories once used as indirect

50

advice." As technology moves Hispanos toward homogeneity, something within them seeks more intense differentiation. The whirlwind of ideas, people, and pop culture reshaping social values makes them uneasy. They worry that what remains of their traditional culture could be lost. Prominent Hispano leaders speak out for more than cultural revival. Their message is one of survival through resistance. Rudolfo Anaya, a prolific Hispano writer, has asked: "Who has taken charge of our lives? We are informed by television, the daily dose of news, the homogeneous school system, and other communication media that are in the hands of the power manipulators" (1993, p. 13). Former Lieutenant Governor Roberto Mondragón urged Hispanos at the 1993 Image of Nuevo Mexico Conference to challenge the influence of Anglo society: "Be bulls. Snort. Stamp. Throw up some dust ... [P]reserve the Spanish language. Because without the language you cannot fully communicate the culture" (Duke, 1993, p. A4).

Caught in the ebb and flow of cultural crosscurrents, Norteño is unsure how to respond to cultural and linguistic erosion. The Norteño community debates about schooling, which are discussed in this chapter, reflect the broader cultural survival controversy among Hispanos throughout the state. Norteños disagree about the role of bilingual education in reviving culture and language in their own community. Should the school district expand the current bilingual programs to include an elementary Spanish developmental program and more secondary subject areas instructed in Spanish? At the heart of the debates is a disagreement about what constitutes the welfare of Norteño's children.

For the past 13 years, Norteño School District administrators have pursued bilingual funds to serve the needs of young Hispanos and Pueblo Indians from low-income families and the 72% of students diagnosed as limited-English-proficient (LEP).[1] The configuration of bilingual programs for Norteño for 1992 to 1993 included a federal transitional program for grades K to 6, a state language maintenance program for grades K to 6 that requires 45 minutes of instruction in

---

[1]Four assessments are used to identify limited-English-proficient students: (a) *Home Language Survey* results indicating that the student's home language is other than English; (b) *Language Assessment Scales (LAS)* results indicating that the student scores below the functional level in English; (c) results from the *Iowa Tests of Basic Skills (ITBS)* indicating that the student scores below the 50th percentile in total reading, language, mathematics, and science; and (d) a teacher's assessment of results from an individually administered rating scale. I participated in administering English language assessment tests for the Norteño Elementary School bilingual program and collated the *Home Language Survey* results.

Spanish per day, and a similar state Spanish language maintenance program in social studies and English classes for grades 7 to 10. The state programs emphasize developing Spanish literacy skills.[2]

In 1993, the administration submitted two new federal bilingual proposals, one to expand the transitional bilingual program to secondary math and science courses, and another to develop an elementary school curriculum taught half in English and half in Spanish. The proposals sparked heated debates throughout the school and community about whether or not bilingual education offers the best approach to meeting the needs of Norteño children.

DEBATE AMONG TEACHERS

I encounter opinions in formal and informal settings, including the high school faculty mailroom, where the debate takes the form of widely distributed newspaper articles. The headline of the first newspaper article to appear in the mailboxes reads: "Bilingual Ed Revives a Threatened Culture." The article reprinted an award-winning essay in a national competition sponsored by the National Association for Bilingual Education. The essay, "Why Bilingual Education Is Important to Me," is an Hispano daughter's reflection about what happened to her mother when students were forbidden to use Spanish in an El Rito classroom:

> "Jessie, if I hear that filth coming from your mouth again I'll wash it out with soap. If you want to speak like that go to Mexico." From this dialogue you would have expected my mother to be speaking profanities. In reality she was caught speaking the only language she knew, Spanish....
>
> In a misguided attempt to protect their children, [Hispanos] refused to speak Spanish at home where the primary language would develop. Once the language is lost, or deliberately forgotten, then the culture is soon to follow. Language is the very pillar of our culture, and without it the walls of our heritage will fall about us. All that will be left for our children is a pile of rub-

---

[2]The following are fieldnotes from a site visit by the bilingual education evaluator from the New Mexico Department of Education about recommendations for improving the Norteño Bilingual Program (22 April 1993):

(1) identify scope and sequence materials to teach Spanish literacy skills; (2) use workbooks sparingly, use more speech communication in activities, get away from the fear of using Spanish with the kids; (3) use the state language maintenance funds to buy materials and to train teachers to use these materials; (4) overcome the tendency to fear materials are too advanced for students; (5) enforce the state requirement of at least 45 minutes of daily instruction in another language (use Spanish to sing songs, give instructions, say the pledge of allegiance).

ble which once represented the pride and unity that our people had....
Bilingual education can prevent this sorry tale from coming to pass. It can
prevent the Hispanic population from being overlooked, and gain for it
some of its long overdue recognition. The days of passive acceptance by the
Hispanic people are over. We are willing to fight for our heritage, our culture. It is a fight we intend to win. (E. Trujillo, cited in "Bilingual Ed Revives," 1993, p. A6)

Some teachers view bilingual education as a way to save kids from the
inevitable assimilation that would occur if the kids only learn the language of the dominant culture; others believe that bilingual education
denies kids a promising economic future. The day after the above essay
appeared in the faculty mailboxes, a rejoinder appears anonymously.
This newspaper article, titled "English Secure as First Language in
U.S.," argues for a common tongue:

The lead story on this week's release of new figures from the 1990 census
was that one out of seven residents of the United States (over the age 5) are
speaking a language other than English at home.... The census results
would seem to indicate that the U.S.A. is becoming diverse to the point of
Balkanization—at least linguistically.... But if you read the fine print, the
census says that better than three out of four of those ESL Americans do
speak English—"well" or "very well." ... We are a nation of immigrants.
People came to America to become Americans, and with a bit of luck to become rich Americans. They still do....

There is going to be continual agitation for bilingualism in the United
States, particularly calls for an English–Spanish system. (More than
one-half of the ESL population speaks Spanish at home.) James Lyons of
the National Association for Bilingual Education says that
"mainstreaming (immigrant) children is unfair, hypocritical and racist."
Aurora Helton, a member of the Oklahoma Hispanic Advisory Committee,
added: "Let's face it. We are not going to be a totally English speaking
country anymore."

Yes, I think we are. We should be. The United States gains a great deal by
having so many languages spoken inside our borders. And the good news
to me is that the immigrants seem to understand that better than some of
their English-articulate spokesmen do. I think these census figures show
that we may be making too much of demands for bilingualism. Aside from
some bilingual help in schools, this should not be a high government priority. People will take care of themselves. They will learn English because
they need it. If they want to speak Spanish or Armenian, they can do that
at home or at the unemployment office. (Reeves, 1993, p. A8)

Supporters of this position view bilingual education as "turning back the clock" and "going back into a mold." One teacher expresses frustration: "Everyone in Norteño is so tied to culture. Is it a fear, or lack of exposure? If we push kids to look at *Chicanismo*,[3] we're doing them a disservice. We can't teach the negativism forever." He goes on to explain that some parents try to force their kids to can food and to plow fields the old way: "Culture is created from necessity, not sentiments. Kids learn what they have to, and they're not going to do things the hard way just because it's traditional."

Few would dispute the merits of providing more jobs for Hispano teachers in the schools, but detractors see a dangerously fine line between increasing ethnic autonomy and returning to isolation. Some fear a trend toward isolation will favor hiring locals and leave students less prepared for the outside world. An Hispano teacher testifies to the growing tension between wanting to prepare the students for change and wanting to preserve the culture:

> I'm upset about this isolationism trend. "Separate but equal" status isn't going to work in this school. By focusing more on who we are, the school is preventing who the students can become. Without outsiders who push at the passivity of the students, they won't learn to think for themselves and to be prepared to face the outside world. I know how hard teachers have to push these kids to form opinions of their own and to think critically. I grew up having to deal with the Anglo world, so I know what kind of exposure these kids need. Culture doesn't stand still. To remove outside influences [in order] to preserve the culture will be the kiss of death to these villages.

The teacher captures the dilemma at its worst, couched in either-or terms: Either promote Hispano tradition and, in the process, encourage a return to isolation, or promote behavior that enables success in the non-Hispano world and, in the process, discourage Hispano tradition.

The same teacher imagines what the future may be like for this region: "Possible federal changes in welfare laws, less employment opportunities at Los Alamos and in the logging business, and low prospects for

---

[3]*Chicanismo* refers to the activism among Mexican Americans against injustice and oppression, for cultural nationalism and self-determination, for the concept of a bilingual and bicultural reality. Rodolfo Acuña (1988) discussed the origins of the Chicano movement in his book *Occupied America: A History of Chicanos*. Armando Trujillo (1996) described how in the 1960s this emergent Chicano worldview affected a Texas school in "In Search of Aztlán: Movimiento Ideology and the Creation of a Chicano Worldview Through Schooling."

industry in Northern New Mexico mean these kids will most likely have to leave for jobs." Will economic history repeat itself, once again forcing Hispanos to scatter to the winds in search of jobs? Raising children to leave is contrary to the local norm of wanting grown children to stay close to home, but this teacher's prediction supports the idea that the school's role in the community is to prepare students for change. Community members who share this teacher's view believe that expanding bilingual education diminishes such preparation.

If approved by the school board, the Norteño School District administration's decision to become more bilingual would have many implications for the faculty. What kind of teaching staff would be best for a K to 12 bilingual program that fits Norteño students? What kind of faculty development would be necessary for current teachers, who came to the school district not being required to teach in Spanish? How should Spanish be integrated into the curriculum—a half day in each language, with the morning lessons repeated in the other language in the afternoon; Spanish specialists rotating between grades K to 12; or simultaneous introduction of concepts in both languages? How should the bilingual program deal with colloquial Spanish?

Bilingual certification requirements jeopardize job security for some teachers and divert others from continuing course work in their content areas or advanced degree programs. Some monolingual teachers fear reassignment, loss of status, or other career setbacks. Several find unrealistic the task of developing bilingual proficiency within the 3-year limit set by the board of education. Native teachers themselves find the written and oral Spanish certification examinations challenging because most have not had formal instruction in standard Spanish vocabulary and grammar.

Adequacy and equity are other critical issues. Teachers complain that the requisite courses for bilingual certification do not adequately prepare them to teach content areas in Spanish. Moreover, an inequity exists between the types of bilingual programs in the elementary and secondary grades. Elementary staff receive full educational benefits— on-site instruction and free tuition—from the federal bilingual program, but secondary teachers are not reimbursed for course work by the state bilingual program and must commute to classes on their own time. The two newly proposed federal bilingual programs would eliminate this discrepancy.

The board of education views the current bilingual programs as assets that bring revenue and teaching assistants to the school, so they frown on teacher complaints about obtaining bilingual certification. The onus falls on the board members to deal with extension requests for the bilingual certification requirements added to faculty contracts. The board president looks at the continuing education requirements as learning opportunities that prepare the faculty to provide understandable instruction that better meets the needs of local students.[4] In response, an Anglo teacher suggests, "It's an admirable goal to be biliterate, but we need to redo the K to 12 curriculum to achieve this rather than require bilingual certification of all teachers."

DEBATE AMONG PARENTS

A Home Language Survey, administered to parents of Norteño's elementary school students, indicates strong parental approval for bilingual education, even though the primary effect is a shift from Spanish to English (see Table 3.1). In response to the question "What language did you speak first?" 28% of the parents answered Spanish. As for the children, only 7% spoke Spanish first. Comparing what language(s) parents and children use at home, a generational change appears. Although 32% of the parents speak only English to their children, 71% of the children speak only English to their parents.

As people of all ages recounted their personal language histories, I realized that the language habits of these individuals depend on a number of factors: place of residence, religious affiliation, the language preference of the extended family, the home language, the spouse's first language, sibling order, gender, occupation, amount of formal Spanish instruction, and the age of the people involved in the conversation. If grandparents live nearby, family members tend to converse more in Spanglish. In large families, older children tend to speak more Spanish because they had more contact with adults during their early years than their younger siblings, who were often left in the care of the older children in the house. Young children from certain villages speak more Spanish than children from other villages do, but even this is changing. Villagers who commute to jobs tend to speak more English than those who work locally or those who live on welfare. The Catholic Church schedules masses throughout the week in Spanish; little Spanish is spoken in the Protestant church.

---

[4]A board member quoted Samuel Betances' definition of bilingual education as "understandable instruction." Dr. Betances, a native of Puerto Rico, is a leader in bilingual education.

TABLE 3.1
1992 Home Language Survey for the Norteño Bilingual Program

	Spanish	English	Both	Total
1. What language did you speak first?	28%	50%	22%	190
2. What language do you speak with your child?	3%	32%	65%	186
3. What language did your child first speak?	7%	80%	13%	190
4. What language does your child speak at home?	4%	71%	25%	191
5. In your opinion, what language(s) is/are important?	0.5%	1.5%	98%	188

	No	Some	Yes	Total
6. Does your child understand English?	0	0	100%	192
7. Does your child understand Spanish?	12%	28%	60%	184

Note. Adapted from the 1992 Home Language Survey administered to parents by the Norteño Elementary Bilingual Program. The parents of 11 Pueblo Indian elementary students wrote in their native language when appropriate. Given that the focus of this study is on the Hispano students, I have not included the Pueblo parents' responses in the survey results.

Middle-aged Norteños grew up during the "cultural deprivation" era that explained low school achievement by minority children in terms of inferior environmental factors. The job of the schools was to overcome the students' disadvantaging culture and native language. I often hear Norteños compare stories of the embarrassment and inadequacy they have felt about speaking English, and of humiliation for being punished when they spoke Spanish. First they were taught not to speak Spanish, then that the colloquial dialect was inferior. Admitting that there are no Spanish reading materials in the house, a parent explains:

> We're battered parents. Probably we're embarrassed by the fact that we don't speak Spanish well after going through the English-saturation program we experienced. We [Hispanics] have the longest tradition of punish-

ing students for speaking their own language; the longest tradition of special education placement for language deficiency; the longest tradition of racially and culturally explaining their failures.

This parent rejects the notion that bilingual education is supposed to build on the students' own cultural background only as a transition into English and American culture. He now supports a bilingual program that emphasizes native language development.

Opinions among faculty and parents do not divide according to social class, insider–outsider, or Anglo–Hispanic categories. Some Anglo parents chose to live in Norteño to expose their children to Spanish; some Hispano parents want their children to learn English well enough to speak without the stigma of an accent, like mainstream Americans. Other Hispano parents teach Spanish as the home language, knowing the children will get instruction in English once they go to school. Some of these parents speak of maintaining a private–public language distinction; others speak of resisting mainstream dominance. One parent conveys the expectation for the young people to carry the cultural torch for generations: "To let the Spanish language die is like giving up your priceless heritage for a tasteless bowl of soup. Keep the Spanish language alive at any cost because in the future we plan to succeed, not only to survive."

Nelson Martínez, a successful Hispano TV anchorman, comes one evening to Norteño as a motivational performer for the elementary school's bilingual program. Afterward, a Norteño mother urges Martínez "to tell the parents to speak to their children in Spanish in order to preserve the language and our culture." He replies, "Learn English first and learn it well. It's the language you have to prove yourself in. Then worry about preserving your culture.... One day the TV station manager asked if I spoke Spanish. Although I didn't speak much Spanish, I said yes and then learned it quickly. Speaking Spanish was my passport to the world.... Leave, learn, and bring back what you've learned to your people."

A graduate of Los Alamos High School, Martínez understands how to compete in the Anglo world. However, his big career break came when TV station managers in Albuquerque assumed that because he has an Hispanic surname, he could speak Spanish. Bilingual news assignments motivated him to develop his Spanish. Becoming successful brought him full circle to appreciating what his Chimayó roots offer him and what he can give in return.

At a regional "Back to School" Family Institute held in September at New Mexico Highlands University (NMHU), parents hear about the pragmatic value of dual language development. Alberto Sandoval, director of NMHU's Bilingual Program, emphasizes that "you don't build by taking away what people have" and urges parents not to relegate Spanish to the home:

> The limits of our world are the limits of our language. Our Spanish in our homes is valuable, but we need to learn formal Spanish. We must develop our Spanish to the same degree as our English, and teach concepts and content areas in Spanish. We must give the Spanish language a degree of utility rather than promote modified assimilation. Through rejection of who you are, you are no one. Here in Northern New Mexico, we have a potential not found anywhere else in the U.S. We haven't capitalized on the potential yet.

A few parents disagree with this utilitarian argument in favor of students' learning Spanish: "How would I have used Spanish in my profession? Why devote the time? Maybe 90% of the students will never use it, so why commit so many educational resources to it? Other than talking to locals or communicating with elders, why?" Another parent emphasizes staying abreast of the mainstream: "Let history be, and do what it takes to live for today."

But there are parents who want the school to sustain the sentiments that maintain community: "Cultural amnesia makes us ignorant of others as well as ourselves." These parents propose that students acquire Hispano cultural knowledge as the basis for future life choices:

> We need to instill as much information as possible into the kids, whether it be culture, history, technology, or anything else. Sooner or later they can make up their own minds. But the kids need to learn all the different avenues, the different things that there are to know. Teaching culture is laying a foundation to come back to. Later in life, children will realize the value of speaking Spanish.

The later-in-life-you'll-come-back-to-your-culture message foreshadows a self-identity for today's Norteño adolescents.

Deciding whether the school district can afford to teach culture brings out a range of viewpoints about the implications of "ethnicizing" public education. Some say, "While our children are growing up is the time to teach them culture. Learn culture in school now and technology later in college." They are countered by those who say, "Culture should be taught at home, technology at school." Opponents of teaching language and cultural heritage do not object to the ideal of learning cultural traditions and speaking Spanish; however, they worry that adding more bilingual programs will dilute the curriculum and jeopardize their children's opportunities to compete outside Norteño. As one parent explains,

> Culture should be taught at home. Mi corazón [my heart] is my family. Culture is the music at home, what we do as a family together—helping Dad dig the acequias, visiting grandma and eating her chile. That's what motivates me to compete. Then it's up to the school to make my kids able to compete.

According to Cecilia Portal, who visits Norteño High School's photography class to discuss her exhibition of Hispano women, "Modern disruptions of traditional lifestyles have led to a separation of generations and the decline of fluency of Spanish spoken in the homes" (personal communication, September 8, 1992). Many parents chose to speak only English to their children because it is "the language to get ahead in," but now some regret not teaching Spanish first. One father admits, "In our home, we speak more English than Spanish. I'm ashamed to say my sons don't speak much Spanish." Guilt and blame abound. Norteño no longer stands as a cultural island, and education paradoxically holds both the hopes of those who look to the future and the hopes of those who look to the past to anchor the lives of the young.

The ambiguity about remaining and becoming—whether to stress the past or the future, or how to accomplish both—has fueled arguments in the community. Who should teach language and culture—the family or the school? Does tradition limit personal growth or provide the basis for it? How should the functions of the school change in response to community changes? At school board meetings about the two federal bilingual proposals, educators and residents disagree strongly about whether learning Spanish in school necessarily revives the cultural knowledge and values of the past. Claims of racism come from Anglos and Hispanos: Anglos feel they are being driven out because they do not speak Spanish; Hispanos view Anglo disapproval as another attempt to reject Hispano ancestry.

DEBATE EPILOGUE

Like bilingual education battles elsewhere, the debates in Norteño stirred deep emotions and split the community. Neighbors and colleagues remember harsh words that were spoken. A few families moved away to ensure the educational experience they preferred for their children; a few sent their children to school in Taos. Most teachers followed the prescribed bilingual certification program.

In regard to the Norteño School District's two federal bilingual proposals, the board of education declined the $200,000 federal grant to fund the dual language immersion program in the elementary school because of the controversy in the community. The policy pendulum swung to the side of becoming—what a school does or hopes to do in the name of change rather than heritage. The board decided that the proposal arrived a generation too late and does not fit the needs of today's Norteño students. The high school math and science bilingual proposal won federal and board approval.

The compromise for the 1993 to 1994 school year included the K to 3 transitional bilingual program, the secondary math and science transitional bilingual program, the K to 6 and 7 to 10 state maintenance programs with 45 minutes of instructional time in Spanish each day, a new Spanish language arts program in the middle school, and more advanced Spanish instruction in the high school. The language arts approach is meant to develop Spanish as a second language rather than as a native language.[5]

Turning down the dual language immersion grant created hard feelings throughout the school district and led to the resignation of Alfonso, the director of the elementary school's bilingual program. During the subsequent election, three incumbent board of education members were defeated by supporters of cultural survival. An incumbent Protestant Hispano's platform for more technology in the school could not compete with the emotional appeal of three more traditional Catholic Hispanos who serve their community as *Penitentes* and wanted the school to preserve the soul of Norteño. One of those *Penitentes* was Alfonso's brother, who ascended to the presidency of the board to rekindle the priority of two cultural cornerstones—language and faith. Once again, board of education meetings began with prayer. Six years later, Alfonso returned with a doctorate in education to serve as superintendent and foster a sense of becoming that sustains strong roots.

---

[5]In 1991, a group of K to 12 teachers wrote a proposal to establish Spanish I and II courses in the secondary school to "help students overcome the provincial feeling that only in English can one conduct an intelligent conversation or discussion" (Norteño School District, 1991). Some students responded to the proposal by requesting other foreign languages besides Spanish.

4

Caught in the Ebb and Flow
of Cultural Crosscurrents

We do not live for a lifetime in the same culture in which we were born nor
in which we will die.... [E]ven if you stay in the same place, the same place
will not stay the same culturally. You become an "immigrant without im-
migrating."
   —Seymour Fresh (Quoted in *Integrating Culture Into the Curriculum*,
   Larry Torres' workshop at Norteño Elementary School)

The advancing and retreating movement of cultures, the increased competition for land and water, and the struggle for cultural dominance in
the region are irrevocably altering Hispano life. The competing claims of
multiple cultural worlds continue to shape who Norteño students are
learning to be, the context of their life experiences inside and outside
school, and their ethnic profiles. Young Norteños today face a different
kind of cultural double bind than their parents faced. According to anthropologist Gladys Levis,

   If [the parents' generation chose] to act like "traditional" Spanish Americans, they [failed] to succeed within the parameters of the Anglo-inspired
   programs. If they [assimilated] to the degree necessary to benefit from the
   programs, then they were operating outside of their own culture and
   [were] liable to social ostracism. (Levis, 1978, p. 5)[1]

Instead of expecting Norteño youth to demonstrate ethnic loyalty by
staying in the community, most parents today expect their children to

---

[1]In her 1978 dissertation *Is there 'something wrong' with Pedregales?* Gladys Levis applied this psychological concept of double bind in her discussion of the impact of assimilation on Hispanos.

leave the community to make something of themselves. At the same time, some ask their children to make a linguistic commitment to their homeland identity.

When I talk with Norteño students about the debate regarding the survival of language and culture, they are unsure how to respond to the cultural crosscurrents pushing and pulling at the their sense of being an Hispano and an American. For these young Hispanos, negotiating ethnicity in Northern New Mexico raises a critical issue: The Norteño heritage is a vanishing facet of American life. No Norteño student disputes this dismal reality, but they disagree about how to respond to it, how to define culture, how to determine which cultural identifiers portray who they are, and how to feel when told they are less Hispanic if they do not speak Spanish.[2]

How do students deal with the expectation that people with Spanish surnames should speak Spanish? Several seniors admit feeling "stupid because we don't know the language when people automatically talk to us in Spanish." Raul laughs as he recounts how an elderly neighbor, associating language with religion, chides him: "When Mr. Gonzales talks to me in Spanish, I answer him in English. He tells me I'll go to hell if I don't speak Spanish." Eliza feels she does not fit the national image of an Hispanic—no dark hair, no dark complexion, no fluency with the Spanish language. She has a Spanish surname and deep regional roots, but she has little knowledge of Norteño agricultural traditions for when she inherits her father's ranch. She is confused: "I don't know how you're supposed to feel when you're an Hispanic." To her elders, being Hispano meant living a certain way in a particular place. Now detached from such a lifestyle, Eliza is not sure how an identifying label and a sense of place should transfer to a sense of being and peoplehood.

The bilingual debate divides students. An editorial in the student newspaper voices a response to the school district's change of policy to require bilingual certification of all faculty. The young journalist asks the readers to consider which has more value for the school, bilingual certification or continuing education in a teacher's subject matter:

> What's the deal with the bilingual program? The object of the bilingual program is to teach students from other countries English where it is

---

[2]Young people in Norteño usually used the ethnic label "Hispanic" and tended to compare themselves to people with Spanish surnames throughout the United States rather than identifying themselves regionally as "Hispanos" or politically as "Chicanos."

needed. While our school encourages teachers to be bilingually certified, I haven't met one student that didn't know English before he or she came here.... I have also heard that several people's jobs are being kept only if they become bilingually certified within a certain amount of time. Teachers should be hired and fired on their teaching ability and not on whether or not they can get a certification that they don't even need. If all we end up with is a bunch of teachers in our school that can't even teach but got hired because they are bilingually certified, then it would be better just to drop out of school.

Did it ever occur to anyone that better time could be spent maybe getting a master's degree in that teacher's field? If the administration feels the need to require a degree in something, they might as well require a degree in something that the teachers need or could use. Save the bilingual stuff for the schools down south that get Mexican immigrants and really need it. Let's just find a way to make our teachers better and quit worrying about this bilingual B.S.

Some students claim that bilingual programs dilute the amount of content they are taught. Alex resents the negative "LEP" (Limited English Proficiency) label on his school records that supports the school's case for seeking bilingual money. He points out a flaw in the compensatory approach of the language transition program: "The bilingual program has been here as long as we seniors have, but our standardized test scores have gotten worse." Teresa, an eighth grader, faces opposition to bilingual education from her grandmother, who learned English at school, not at home. Teresa explains, "Trying to learn concepts and terms in both languages only confused her when she was my age." But the bilingual program has student supporters. Martina thinks teaching in two languages will do a lot of good:

> I think it would bring back what's been lost. I know it would help me a lot. But the teachers are going to have to go at a slower pace, because a lot of the students understand Spanish but cannot say a word to save their life. I don't think learning about our culture is turning the clock back.

In a wishful conclusion, Martina adds, "Everything will be going forward as everybody goes back to their culture." Clearly, she wants both progress and traditions, and wanting both, she does not consider how they might be at odds with each other.

A language gap occurs between school and home. Teachers complain that parents are not reinforcing Spanish at home; parents explain that their generation lacks the fluency and Spanish literacy skills necessary to help their children; students claim that their families do not speak the "right" Spanish. According to a junior,

> When I started taking Spanish this year, I had a hard time at the beginning because my grandparents use a lot of Spanglish. There's a lot of slang because everything gets changed. I learned things differently from the proper Spanish, so now I'm trying to adjust to the right way to speak.

Some linguists worry that teaching textbook Spanish to speakers of the local Spanish may correct student "errors" but not advance proficiency as a whole (Valdés, 1981, 1997).[3]

A language gap exists between the generations. When grandparents address their grandchildren in Spanish and the young respond in English, the lack of a mutual language prevents a full dialogue. Some grandparents get upset when grandchildren do not talk in Spanish; they fear the loss of the cultural wisdom that only Spanish conveys. Aurelio, a sophomore, regrets losing touch with his grandparents:

> It seems like we don't care enough about our grandparents to ask them questions or be around them enough. We just care about how we feel and what we want to do. When you're young, it seems like you don't really want to think about history or your ancestors and what they did, so you kind of just ignore it. Later on, when we're more mature, I'm sure we'll probably regret not learning to speak the language or more about where we came from.

Pondering the language barrier she has with her grandparents, a senior named Delores describes how she came to not speak much Spanish:

> Although my grandparents understand and speak English, I feel embarrassed and uncomfortable not being able to relate anything back to them in Spanish. I'm just embarrassed by the fact that I've never learned. Nobody took the time to teach me to speak Spanish. Nobody ever told me, "Delores, don't speak Spanish. We don't want you to learn how to do it." I

---

[3]Guadalupe Valdés (1981, 1997) studied the pedagogical problems of teaching Spanish to Hispanophone bilinguals as compared to teaching Spanish as a foreign language to Anglophone students. Some Hispanophone students exhibit minimal competencies, understanding only everyday Spanish related to a limited number of topics. Others may read and write Spanish. See *La Enseñanza del español a Hispanohablantes: Praxis y teoría* (Colombi & Alarcón, 1997) for information about identifying Hispanophone students and their needs, models of applied linguistics for teaching them Spanish, and suggestions for improved teaching practices.

just never did. They talked to me in Spanish, and I talked back in English.
Now my parents realize the error of their ways.

Another high school student wrote about this shift in language use in
a report comparing four generations of women in her family:

Great-grandmother: The language spoken more often was Spanish. English
was rarely spoken.

Grandmother: Spanish was spoken at home. English was sometimes
spoken at school.

Mother: The language my mother spoke more often was English. The only time she would speak Spanish was when
she would talk to her grandparents. She regrets not
learning Spanish that well, because she has trouble saying a lot of words now that she is older.

Me: Both English and Spanish are spoken at home. Young
people have their own "slang," which most parents do
not understand.

In addition to this generational swing in home language use, a gap exists in some of the family histories. Reading essays from an eighth-grade
English assignment about *Su Padre* [Your Father], I noted that nearly
50% of the students' fathers were born elsewhere, because the grandparents had left Norteño in search of work. The absence of these fathers
from Norteño during their own formative years has contributed to some
of the cultural discontinuity facing the community. The returnees face
ridicule for not speaking Spanish fluently and for "being too Anglo." One
father wrote about the fragile self-esteem that comes from being caught
between the two cultural worlds:

What does it take to be accepted in the Anglo world? Education? No, under
the degrees, it still feels like it would only take one misstep—one ignorant
statement to bring the whole house of cards falling down.... [N]o matter
how healthy our self-esteem, it is fragile, indeed, susceptible to the least
suggestion of negative criticism. Perhaps one can be accepted only among
one's own—except now you talk differently, think differently, want different things for your family—seeking to blend, to blend in, to blend out. But
they will take you back, if you are patient and wait and don't push, and
prove yourself, they will take you back. But like a faithless lover, there will
always be a little doubt.

The migrations of past generations have touched the lives of many
students. Perhaps the young worry less about acceptance because Span-

ish was not originally part of their identity. Most students have felt occasional embarrassment about not being able to speak Spanish. However, they disagree about the relationship between the loss of language and the loss of culture. The following comments represent the breadth of student opinions about the value of the Spanish language. Those who feel anxious about the loss say:

> The local Spanish language is being lost. It's like someone's dying. Once it dies off, we're not going to be able to learn it again. What will I have to pass on to my children?

> Our historical roots are lost with the loss of language.

> I intend to make sure my kids don't forget their native language or roots.

Some cannot relate to their parents' sense of urgency about preserving language and culture:

> What do I need to speak Spanish for? I can't wait to leave this place.

> My father tells me to listen to Spanish music instead of rock and heavy metal, because it's our culture. My grandparents tell me I've got to speak Spanish, but I say I don't need it right now. It won't have any impact on my life right now, so why would I want to do something that's going to waste my time or be useless to me?

Some view language as only one cultural characteristic among many others that are more firmly anchored in historical reality:

> Culture is bigger than just language.

> Hispanic identity runs deep in New Mexico's history, so it's not dependent on just language.

One student expresses a more pragmatic attitude about speaking Spanish:

> I'm studying Spanish to get jobs.

Part of this disagreement about cultural maintenance stems from the students' notion of culture. In response to their teacher's request for a definition of culture, seventh graders replied: a way of living, *chicos* [dry corn] and *tortillas*, having a baby and raising it like you, carrying on traditions like language. The answers ran the gamut from viewing culture as a birthright and a process of socialization to eating certain food and doing things a certain way.

Talking with older students, I learn that their definitions of culture center on the issue of identity and culture as objects of the past. They confuse culture with traditions. Culture has become an explicit topic taught in school rather than an implicit part of everyday life. Michael, a senior, describes culture as his heritage, rather than a way of life:

> The older people were deeper in their culture, living off the land. Back then they didn't think of it as culture. It was just a way of life—the Hispanic way. And now we think of it as culture. I'm studying my culture in school, but I haven't lived it. My grandparents lived it. Ethnicity is a decoration now, not a way of life.

> It's hard in today's society to keep your culture. Even in our parents' days, they didn't have a culture. They didn't have ethnicity. They had a way of life. What we call today our culture, our being Hispanic, is just what they lived every single day.

Andrea, another senior, echoes Michael's sentiment about culture being a former way of life that cannot be duplicated. She also sees her ethnicity as an accessory:

> It's fun to be Spanish. It's a recreational kind of thing, and we can invite friends to things that we do. Culture shouldn't be who you are, like your only identity. I shouldn't introduce myself as "Hi, I'm Andrea. I'm Hispanic." I should just be me—who I am, not who my parents were, not where I was born or anything like that. It's really irrelevant. Culture is not something I carry into my work or anything. It's not something that's necessary to be successful in life.

From Andrea and Michael's perspectives, culture plays a minor role in modern life; it is a flavoring rather than the main ingredient. The culture that served Andrea's grandparents' needs no longer serves hers. The remote reality of their grandparents' culture gives these students the impression that culture is only relevant as a way to distinguish two groups of people—Hispanos and Anglos—once separated geographically and linguistically. The Hispano fabric of their lives is not as apparent to them as it is to their elders.

Should the school teach about the culture? Students do not agree:

> **Juan:** Yes, I think it would be very valuable, because not knowing is kind of hard. There's a void, an emptiness.
>
> **Leroy:** No, it should be brought up in the house by the parents. Culture needs to be introduced, shared, and appreci-

ated, but left at that. You shouldn't be forced to speak
Spanish or taught only how to make Spanish foods.
Melissa: Culture should be taught at home, but you shouldn't be
forced to leave it at home when you come to school.
That's a part of you that goes with you wherever you go.
I think they should build on it in school, instead of just
saying forget it.

Students grasp the public versus private individuality dichotomy. They
agree that culture is an essential part of one's private individuality, but
they disagree about where the boundaries of ethnicity should be drawn.
Leroy draws a clear line between home and school; Melissa feels school
should reinforce what students learn at home; Juan recognizes the need
to learn something he is missing at home. How should the schools respond to this "betweenness" Norteño children express about their ethnic socialization?

ETHNIC IDENTITY VERSUS ETHNIC IDENTIFICATION

Formal education places a premium on learning by reading rather than
by living, listening, and observing. The written word can preserve what
"could be lost forever as easily as one generation is lost to the next, as
easily as one old man might lose his voice, having spoken not enough or
not at all" (Momaday, 1966, p. 178). But when the primary method of
transmitting culture is through books and performance rather than
through lived experience, the culture is in trouble. Words dilute and fail
to capture the culture's way of being; they present a static concept of culture. Culture thrives on repetition, attachment to daily life, and intimacy. As culture becomes merely heritage, a matter of the past tense,
ethnic labeling shifts. Ethnic identity—an individual process of defining
and establishing Who am I?—declines, and ethnic identification—a simpler social process that asks What am I?—takes its place. Ethnic identification is more a perception of belonging rather than an awareness of
being (Hayes-Bautista, 1974).

As ethnic labeling for Norteño youth becomes more attached to place
rather than lifestyle, the quest for cultural reaffirmation includes adapting and adopting traditions that bond the individual to the community
through faith. With the decline in Holy Week pilgrimages to the
Santuario in far-off Chimayó, *Las Guadalupanas*, a women's religious
group, started the ritual of a Good Friday pilgrimage. *Peregrinos* [pil-
grims] walk about 7 miles from Norteño's Catholic Church through sev-

eral villages, sharing the burden of carrying a *madero* [heavy wooden cross] and stopping to visit the saints at the pueblo's church and the *morada* [Penitente chapel] near the school. The long line of pilgrims includes children and teenagers who are active in the Catholic Church.

In addition, the aging *Penitentes* are again attracting young men to be keepers of the community's faith and functioning more openly as a part of village life. During Holy Week's commemoration of the Passion of Jesus, all rituals and hymns are in Spanish, and some ceremonies for nonmembers now take place in the Catholic Church as well as the *morada*. Although the language eludes most of the young who attend, the sentiment envelops them.

Some educators actively encourage young people to preserve community traditions through the Catholic Church. The elementary school principal, who serves as the director of Norteño's Catholic youth choir, often chooses Spanish songs for Sunday mass. For Christmas 1992, the principal selected "Los Pastores," a traditional morality play, for his group to perform in Spanish. Some students needed cue cards and seemed unsure of the significance of the play, but all agreed to do the play on behalf of the community elders. The principal, who attended New Mexico State University in the southern part of the state, held a *quinceañera* for his stepdaughter when she was 15 years old to mark her symbolic wedding to the Catholic Church. This Mexican tradition, along with celebrating *Cinco de Mayo*, is a newcomer to the Norteño cultural scene. Why introduce traditions not from Northern New Mexico? The bilingual director explains, "Probably only 5 to 10% of the students will stay in Northern New Mexico. They need to be exposed to what they'll encounter away from here as Hispanics."

The social presentation of ethnicity for Norteño youth today depends on a broader range of intercultural contact and a more limited knowledge of cultural context than previous generations experienced (Davidson, Yu, & Phelan, 1993).[4] Because of more intercultural "mingling," this generation seems not to feel the cultural double bind that marginalized their parents in the 1970s (Peshkin, 1991).[5] The no-win situation of yesterday has a new twist—more tolerance for diversity, more

---

[4]Ann Locke Davidson, Hanh Cao Yu, and Patricia Phelan (1993) developed the notion of "social presentation of self" to try to understand what political and relational factors characterize school settings and how students respond to these contexts. In "The Ebb and Flow of Ethnicity: Constructing Identity in Varied School Settings," they suggested the theme of advancing and retreating movement of cultures that is developed in this book.

[5]Alan Peshkin (1991) reported how students in a multiethnic school in California used the term "mingling" to discuss intercultural interactions in *The Color of Strangers, The Color of Friends: The Play of Ethnicity in School and Community.*

mainstream opportunities, more acceptance of biculturalism. Being Norteño no longer means just staying in the village and living the traditional lifestyle. In fact, a school aide said she encountered criticism for staying. One can now enter the mainstream and retain one's cultural identity; however, a tension persists between choosing socioeconomic success outside the community over the fulfillment that comes from the sense of belonging in the community.

A consistent message from teachers addresses this outward-bound orientation: "Remember who you are, where you're from, and the great value you have to offer others." Many students talk of leaving to see the world, but of perhaps returning to raise a family. Their ethnic identity extends beyond the village limits: "Being Hispanic makes me feel unique. I have something to show for what I am." But one student cautions her peers about ethnic identity: "I don't believe in the victimization myth that blames Anglos for the poorer conditions of Hispanics. If you fail or encounter barriers, it's because of who you are or aren't."

The generation gap widens as a concession to the 1990s. While the parents revere the simpler way things were, the young seek the latest fads and material comforts. As one senior puts it, "School and television pull you to material things." Eighth graders wrote about themselves—"what I am, like, want, hate, love, need, and try to do":

Carmen: I want a car of my own someday, just to get around. I want a good, high-paying job. I want a good, rich husband and family. I want a bigger room. Finally, I want to move away from this sleepy, old, small, forever boring town.

Vicente: This summer I went to a [lowrider] car show. It was more of an Hispanic show than a car show. This was called the Raza Tour. Raza is an Hispanic woman that talks about our heritage. She says that it's okay to have a lowrider, but never lose your heritage. I want a lot of new stuff, but my dad doesn't want to buy it because he is afraid I will lose my heritage. But I never will, no matter what.

Alex: When I get out of high school, I plan to become a veterinarian. I want to come back to [my village] and set up my office, so it will help all the local people. This will be a real help to my dad. I hope to inherit his farm one day.

Monica: I want to accomplish graduating from high school with some kind of honor and get a scholarship to go to a good

college to get my master's degree. After that, I want to
move to a big city and start a career at being a mathematical engineer that gets paid good money and gets
rich.

Joe: Success to me is having a job that I enjoy, doing something that I enjoy doing, making the type of money that
I want to make, and having everything I need or want.

These students' definition of self centers on what they hope to do and
to have—their choices in occupation and consumption. Vicente does not
understand his father's concern that Vicente will be lost in a throwaway
culture. All these students plan to leave to make something of themselves. Alex hopes to bring back something to offer his community;
Monica sees education as a one-way ticket out.

Parents see their children as "the last hope" for the culture, but few
students really understand the politics of identity and resistance.
Growing up in the majority, few Norteño youths have a position to speak
from. Cultural congruence between the community and school camou-
flages the cultural discontinuity outside the community. Resistance
makes little sense in a classroom where the teacher is a relative or in a
school where most of the employees come from one's own community.

Norteño adolescents struggle to understand the main forces at work
in their lives, but few recognize the cultural forces, much less the retreating and advancing movement of the cultures. A fine line exists between culture that anchors identity and culture that holds back change.
As the young flow in the direction of the Anglo culture, the parents are
trying to make the movement bidirectional. The parents tend to view
ethnic identity as a cluster of selves—who you have been, who you are,
who you will be. The youth seem to see ethnic identity more as who your
ancestors were. Norteño adolescents once lived within the culture. Today they are living between and sometimes outside of two cultures—isolated from one geographically and the other linguistically.[6]

CUENTOS AND CONSEJOS: STORIES AND ADVICE

The altering meaning of ethnicity for Norteño children is a function of
continual change in their immediate environment, in the sociocultural
context of their community, and in relationships within and outside their

---

[6]José Antonio Burciaga (1993) illustrated the ironies of living within, between, and
sometimes outside of two cultures in *Drink Cultura: Chicanismo.*

community. To understand the implications of change on the life choices of people in Norteño, I asked young and old to tell their stories about what's not present in the lives of young people today that was present in the lives of the elders, and what's present today that wasn't before.

I obtained additional insight from assisting the creative writing teacher with interview training and transcript feedback to students for their family oral history projects. I also designed a multivocal writing project, which an eighth-grade English teacher incorporated into her curriculum (see Table 4.1). Through this project, the students created intergenerational stories about culture in motion that allowed me to understand some of the conditions and consequences of change in Norteño.

The following *cuento* [story] about the Anaya family is my composite of what people across three generations said and wrote about life choices and circumstances. Through storytelling, I hope to illustrate the complexity of remaining and becoming in an intergenerational context with differences Norteños voiced about daily domestic routines, schooling experiences, lifestyle preferences, language use patterns, attitudes toward modernization, and religiousness. This textual experimentation incorporates data into a dramatic dialogue, in which the voices of students, parents, and grandparents are juxtaposed; it is meant to highlight some of the differences between their respective experiences and outlooks (Coffey & Atkinson, 1996).[7]

My intent is neither to stereotype Norteño families nor to lament change. The nostalgia expressed by the elders should neither demean nor romanticize the old ways. Their disapproval of some of the changes conveys their feelings and perceptions about the substance of community change.[8] *Consejos* attached to everyday conversation offer spontaneous homilies to guide *la educación* [the moral education] of the family (Delgado-Gaitan, 1994; Valdés, 1996). The Anaya's home life includes images of various homes where I enjoyed good hospitality; their daily life includes images of school and community routines I observed.

Storytelling connects the past, present, and future. Cultural narratives convey feelings, perceptions, beliefs, actions, and responses to life.

---

[7]I am indebted to the students, teachers, parents, and grandparents who critiqued drafts of this allegory, which holds bits of their wisdom and families' stories about the ambiguity of losses and gains.

[8]In *No Lloro Pero Me Acuerdo*, Josephine Córdova (1976) portrayed the sentiments of elderly Hispanos about the changes their communities and families were experiencing. The elderly were remembering, not crying about, the past.

TABLE 4.1

Multivocal Generations Writing Assignment

"Multivocal Story"

Multivocal writing brings several voices together to tell a story from various points of view. In order to represent the points of view of others, you need to interview the significant people whose voices you want to include.

"Generations Story"

Compare yourself to your same-sex parent and same-sex grandparents. Consider the similarities and differences in how you have all grown up. How are you alike? How are you different?

Questions to help you develop your Generations Story:

1. What has and what has not changed in the lives of people growing up here over the past generations?
   - family life
   - community life
   - school life
   - gender roles
   - language
   - ethnic identity
   - values
   - leisure activities
   - options
2. What is present and what is not present in the lives of young people that was present in the lives of my parents and grandparents?

Suggestions for how to write a Multivocal Story:

1. Write about how you have become who you are and include the voices of those whose messages influenced you along the way.
2. Chronologically retell an event as different people remember it.
3. Compare and contrast the childhoods of the three generations. What is the same? What has changed? How are you alike? How are you different?
4. Create imaginary diary entries or letters of correspondence between you and the other people whose lives touched yours in some way.

They express common experiences or observations, rules for living a healthy life, compelling motives, vague aspirations, or some bit of folk wisdom. Stories often shape, rather than simply reflect, human conduct because they embody intentions. Such *cuentos* illustrate that people make their own histories, but often under conditions not of their own choosing, and with consequences they did not intend (Rosaldo, 1989).[9]

* * *

Julie waits impatiently for the curling iron to warm up, while her younger brother Leroy shouts through the bathroom door for her to hurry up. Their parents commute daily to Los Alamos, leaving each morning before the children wake up. Samuel is an ironworker; Delfiña takes care of purchase orders for the laboratories. Julie can hear her grandmother, Matilda, in the next room answering little Jacob's incessant questions as she dresses him. In the bathroom mirror, a succession of faces stare back at Julie. Her mother's gaze holds her daughter's, each trying to see herself in the other. In place of a curling iron, Delfiña rolls her hair on spongy curlers to sleep on overnight. Behind Delfiña stands a young image of Grandma in the 1930s, curling her hair by wrapping clumps in homemade strips of thin tin.

Matilda grew up without electricity or the time to bother with her hair in the morning, except for Sundays. As soon as the sun came up, her father would wake her by pulling on her feet. "Come on. Come on. The wind is already blowing." As she awakens her grandchildren, she remembers how she felt when her sleep was interrupted by this familiar tug. In her day, Matilda would have fed the cows and chickens and milked the goat before breakfast. By 6:00 she was walking the 6 miles to school.

Around the kitchen are all the ingredients for the special foods Matilda always cooks during Holy Week—*panocha, torta de huevo, sopa, verdolagas, chicos.* The habit of cooking large quantities stays with the old woman, for *Semana Santa* used to be a time when families gathered and neighbors sent children to each other's homes and to the *moradas* with bowls of food. She notes with a sigh that many of the foods and customs have slowly disappeared in the last 30 years of "progress," busy schedules, jobs, and fast foods.

Drawn by the familiar morning smells and sounds of frying eggs and potatoes, Julie hurries to the kitchen. Grandma prefers to cook on the woodstove to conserve on butane costs for the oven. Julie takes a fresh homemade tortilla off the top of a stack and kisses Grandma while cir-

---

[9]In *Culture and Truth: The Remaking of Social Analysis*, Renato Rosaldo (1989) explained that social analysts interested in the interplay of *structure* and *human agency* question how social life is both inherited and always being changed.

cling the table. The old ones prefer speaking Spanish—"*Buenos días le dé Dios, mi hijita*—God grant you a good day, my child." The young ones, English—"Good morning, Grandma." Julie's grandparents seem confused by the grandchildren's insistence on responding in English, but for many of the teenagers, Spanish is just a subject in school. Now that the parents work in Los Alamos and speak English all day, they don't switch back into Spanish much at home.

"Grandma, how is Grandpa?" Pedro Antonio is already at the chicken coop, a vestige of his life of chores. Julie worries about him. If he dies, what part of her will die with him? "My life is a luxury cruise to the Bahamas compared to Grandpa's. Maybe he's right when he tells me that things come too easy to kids today." On the other hand, Pedro Antonio worries about his grandchildren's stressful lives with more difficult schoolwork, raised expectations, greater job competition, peer pressure, and other distractions. Pedro Antonio is proud of his grandchildren yet somewhat uneasy about the turn their lives are taking. Grandpa disapproves of all the time kids spend away from their families. He often advises his grandkids to pray more and not to forget their language or where they're from.

Julie looks apologetically at Matilda. "Grandma, are you still mad at me for eating a bologna sandwich during Lent?" To put some faith back in the girl, Matilda made her kneel by the *santos* for an hour of contemplation. Matilda frets about the loss of faith. The more people have, the less grateful they feel to God. She complains, "People don't stop working during Holy Week like they used to. And they've forgotten how to respect the dead. Last week Compadre Juan's body wasn't even cold when his nephews left the cemetery with the radio blaring. Mourning used to be a time of prayer and solemn remembrance, but you kids can't imagine a year without music." Matilda wonders why the young no longer fear the final judgment if they are disobedient.

Before running to catch the bus, Julie checks the wood box to make sure there's enough *leña* there to keep the stove stoked until she comes home. She yells at Leroy not to forget his guitar, and they depart, leaving the house to the youngest and oldest. The bus swings by Tia Carmela's house to pick up their younger sister, Francella. Every night the children take turns sleeping with their aunt, who lives alone.

Matilda surveys the house to decide what to clean first. Her eyes pause at the family's Spanish coat of arms hanging prominently on the thick living room wall, one of the original adobe walls her father built. Anaya roots run deep in the valley. She picks up each of the framed family photos, slowly wiping them as she rehearses the names of her 19 grandchildren. Each name is a page in her history; each recalls the older namesake. Holding her parents' photo up to the light, she whispers, "You didn't get to rest when you were alive, so you're resting now." With a reverent touch, she removes the dust from the pictures of saints, Our Lady of Carmel, and the many crucifixes on the wall. Passing by Leroy and Jacob's room, she shakes her head in disapproval at the Michael Jordan posters on the walls and the clutter of sports equipment and toys. The basketball star seems a long way from home in Norteño, where so much of the outside world is at once both familiar and strange.

How simple diversions used to be when they wrapped strips of cloth in a tight ball to play stickball and cut up mail-order catalogs to make paper dolls. She smiles at the memory of flipping through the catalog pages, dreaming of owning all the pretty things she saw. With 14 mouths to feed, the family had no extra money for store-bought toys. Her grandmother made Matilda's dolls out of flour sacks, and her brothers played with cars made of thread spools or sardine cans. She mused, "I was fed by grandfather's land and clothed by grandmother's skillful sewing hands. I have built my own dreams out of those things that were so much a part of my childhood."

There's so much laundry to be washed. She turns around, speaking to Grandpa in Spanish as he walks slowly into the kitchen for a cup of coffee: "If these kids had to haul water from the ditch, heat it over a cookstove, and scrub with a washboard, they'd think twice about having so many clothes! All they do is push a button on a machine—no hassle, no stress, no physical labor." Pedro Antonio nods in agreement and sits down. When he was young, he only had one set of clothes for school, for work. New shoes were expensive, so he had to repair his old ones with pieces of scrap leather and cardboard.

Over the years, Pedro Antonio asked much of his body as he tended sheep in the mountains of Wyoming, repaired railroad tracks for the Denver Rio Grande Railroad, and built additions to the family's adobe house every 8 months when he'd return to Norteño. He suffered from a back injury while working in the Silver King mineral mine in Utah. During the Great Depression, Pedro Antonio worked for the Civilian Conservation Corps for a dollar a day. Being too old for the draft in World War II, he worked in a California shipyard. Sometimes he took his children to Colorado to pick potatoes, but he hated to labor on property he would never be able to will to his children.

The family's nine-room house had once been the two-room house Matilda was born in. Her parents slept in one room; their 12 children slept on mattresses in the other. Looking around the house, Pedro Antonio takes pride in what his hands have added to the family legacy. But he frowns as he sips his coffee. *"Vieja,"* he calls to his wife, "Vicente told me about the new taxes on this place. He says they've gone up from $50 to $450 because the Anglos now value adobes. How can a house I built out of dirt for nothing but sweat be worth so much?"

Flattening tortilla dough between her hands, she replies, "They say that property taxes are going up because people are selling their land for big money to the Californians and Texans, who think they're getting a deal for a house with land for only $150,000. Did you know that the Padillas are buying back the land their brother sold to some Texans?"

His grip tightens on the mug as he answers, "We are nothing without our land. Money disappears quickly, but land is always with you. That's why I put in our will that our land can only be sold to family." Sipping his coffee, Pedro Antonio watches Matilda move around the kitchen. Even at 74, she is a handsome woman. How could such a petite woman have carried on her head basket-loads of dirt from the hillside to plaster the house? All those years that the need for cash took her husband away from home, the fruits of Matilda's labor kept them fed. Farm chores marked the seasons. Animals supplied meat, milk, eggs, butter, lard, and soap. The *soterrano*, dug into the hillside, stored the canned vegetables from the large garden she planted, and the *carne seca* and dried fruits—apples, apricots, cherries, pears—lasted all winter. In the course of their lives, Pedro Antonio and Matilda have demonstrated their capacity for survival, faith, hard work, and loyalty.

At school, Julie mingles with friends in the commons area before classes start. Photos of alumni look down from the walls as students stretch out on carpeted steps, comparing gossip about who is going with whom to prom. Groups congregate: Anglo boys play hackey sack, jocks with letterman jackets joke around with the girls, drill team members discuss their new *Yo No Sé* routine for Saturday's game, and Leroy hangs out by the pop machine with the metal head guys who wear black jackets and heavy metal band T-shirts. One boy asks the library assistant for a screwdriver to fix the water fountain: "Grandma, no tiene un Phillips?"

As Julie heads off to her Communication Skills class, the counselor stops her: "Remember that today is the deadline to sign up for summer programs." So many choices—Upward Bound, the Forest Service's Minority Outreach-Education-Employment camp, the Minority Introduction to

Mineral Engineering and Science program, or Project I Teach, which tries to recruit minorities into education. Last summer Julie attended the National Hispanic Institute in Albuquerque and felt uncomfortable with all the *Viva La Raza* talk—how her people have been downtrodden for so many years. Ironically, her best friends are Anglos and she's never felt discriminated against, but her cousins in Albuquerque tease her about being naive: She grows up part of a majority in Norteño.

Delfiña urges her children to take advantage of these special programs, because such programs didn't exist when she was their age. For her, on-the-job training had to suffice. Because she was the eldest of 10, going to college was unrealistic. Affirmative action, Pell Grants, and academic scholarships came too late for her. So she often tells Julie and her other children, "Education is the ticket to a great life and to making it anywhere. Be a leader, not a follower. Fill your dreams and carry your own load in life. We'll be close by if you stumble under the burden."

Next year Julie will be eligible to work in the Los Alamos Co-Op Program, which would allow her to go to school mornings and work afternoons at the labs. Two students participate in the program this year. Mr. Ortiz, the recruiter from Los Alamos National Laboratories, told the students that people from Northern New Mexico used to be hired as the grunts to do the pick-and-shovel work. Now the labs bring in Hispano students to be administrative aides and research assistants. Julie knows that if she gets a foot in the door, she could eventually find a permanent job there and stay in Norteño. But Julie feels the pull of the outside world tugging against her roots.

Samuel, her dad, knows his children will probably need to leave to make something of themselves. He hopes their roots will remain sufficiently intact so they will come back someday. So he takes them often to the cemetery and tells them about his great-great-grandmother who is buried there. In his cautionary way, he says, "I've met so many people in Los Alamos who don't think anything of moving. When I ask them where their family is from, they usually say, 'All over.'"

At school, daily announcements are read aloud in first period: "Congratulations to the students in Business Professionals of America (BPA) who competed Saturday. Julie Anaya took first place in computer applications and extemporaneous communications." With the money BPA students have earned from candy sales, Julie's going with the sponsor to Washington, DC to compete in the nationals.

Julie's sophomore class has spent 2 weeks in Communication Skills learning about getting a job. They have been practicing job interview skills in front of a video camera. The students filled out applications for jobs that their previous work experience qualified them for and wrote résumés and cover letters. Homemade job vacancy posters cover the walls: a nanny for Mother Goose Child Care, a salesperson for Flowers of the Desert, a delivery person for a pizza parlor. Mrs. Smith tells the students that she will judge body language, posture, and quality of voice in the interviews. Points will be deducted for inappropriate attire, she warns them.

In jeans and a cowboy hat, Julie's classmate Arthur applies to be a horse trainer. He hopes to become a professional rider. Bernadette wants to be a cashier in a record store to earn money to study biology at Notre Dame. Her dream is to combine career and family. Bruce is applying to be a Los Alamos lab assistant, because he eventually wants to get a doctorate in math or science from the Massachusetts Institute of Technology. Julie is interviewing for a secretarial position. She anticipates being asked about her long-term goals: to go to college, become president of a business, get married, have two children, and own a house.

After school, Leroy shoots hoops while waiting for Julie to finish track practice. Ever since Julie's legs grew long enough to hop over the acequias, her father has been coaching her long jumping. Samuel trained in high school by jumping across the wide stream that runs through their property:

> At first I always landed in the water, but eventually I made dry landings on the other bank.

Samuel also loves basketball, and he laughs when he tells his son how kids used to play the game before the village gym was built:

> We had to sweep the snow off the outdoor court and wait for the sun to come out and dry the dirt. When we would travel to other communities where they had gyms, we weren't used to playing with a ceiling. We'd pass and shoot the ball too high, hitting the ceiling, or lose control of the ball, because it bounced higher on the hard floor.

Before going home for dinner, Leroy and Julie walk to the Catholic Church for a youth group meeting of COOL—Christ Owns Our Lives. Leroy is rehearsing his role in a skit about alcoholism to be performed at the Southwest Charismatic Conference in Albuquerque. He plays the part of a boy whose father suffers from alcoholism, a problem often found in the Norteño community. The son finally gets his father to let the compassion of Christ into his life in order to find the strength to change. The last priest in Norteño brought the charismatic movement to Norteño. The kids invited their grandmother to hear the musical testimonials of the Benavides family. The clapping, singing, and hugging didn't mesh at all with Matilda's notion of church as a quiet place for prayer.

As Julie and Leroy near the house, they spot little brother Jacob outside with Grandpa. The two are huddled over a pile of dirt with a stick standing in the middle. Jacobo, as Grandpa prefers him to be called, proudly points to their homemade sundial. Grandpa doesn't like his grandchildren's Anglo names and insists his never be Anglicized. He too takes pride in the sundial, but his regard for it comes more from sharing the work with Jacobo than from the novelty of their creation. He misses the lifestyle that kept family members and neighbors working side by side. The rush to make money leaves parents little time to be at home, so Grandpa has taken on the responsibility of teaching respect and discipline. He considers some young people *mal criados*—raised without manners or knowing how to treat people.

At times Grandpa gets on Samuel's case about how materialism has changed their way of life:

The dollar has taken over where giving a hand used to be.

Pedro Antonio regrets both the false sense of independence that money gives and the way money affects how time is spent:

Samuel, your children take care of the chickens, cows, and horses like I did growing up, but their time spent outdoors competes with Nintendo, a stereo, and CDs. I spent lots of time outdoors thinking about life, how the soil was turned. Now, there's no time to think.

Pedro Antonio was brought up to appreciate the land and the way it can be worked by one's own hands. To him, it's better to have less and not be at the mercy of wants.

Valuing education, Samuel's parents sent their two oldest sons to Albuquerque to attend Menaul, a Presbyterian boarding school. Going away to this non-Catholic school created baggage: not fitting in when home for vacations, being perceived as "feeling superior." Samuel watched the social gap grow between his brothers and the community, so he chose not to follow their lead. After high school, Samuel worked a few years at a sawmill and for the highway department before being drafted. The military was his first experience away from home; he is the first to admit how afraid he was of getting lost beyond the gates of the base. Never before did he have to speak English all the time, be with people of other ethnic backgrounds, or feel the stings of prejudice. After using the GI Bill to attend trade school, Samuel got into the ironworkers union with the help of a *compadre*. Commuting allows him to stay in the community but leaves little time for visiting or entertaining the family.

Grandpa scolds the family for not being neighborly, and as they pass graffiti sprayed on the wall of an abandoned building, he says:

> When we were poor, we got along better. There was less *envidia*—envy or selfishness. We shared what little we had, like making *chicos* in the *horno*. We gathered neighbors together to roast all of ours. Same with hoeing gardens. For *matanzas*, we took turns slaughtering and sharing our livestock with neighbors—a great way to have fresh meat more often in the days of no refrigeration. People today search for life in the fast lane of education, money, and opportunity—the new Trinity.

Guilt gnaws at Samuel, for he feels caught between two worlds, two generations:

> You're right. We've lost many of the old traditions in the name of convenience. But Pedro Antonio, have you forgotten the burden of poverty—the struggles of working for Anglo *patrones* who didn't respect you, the layoffs, the painful goodbyes every time you left your family? The rat race at least allows me to live where my heart is and give my children more than I had. No more moving from place to place, finding odd jobs here and there, or buying clothes and toys at secondhand stores. I never want their bodies to ache like ours do.

But Pedro Antonio fears there is a harsher poverty now: People no longer own themselves.

* * *

For Pedro Antonio and Matilda's generation, life was sustained by the ethos of family: caring and sharing, hard work, respect, discipline. Being a good person, a good neighbor, once distinguished a successful Norteño; the only poverty was lack of character. A wealth of facts was no substitute for meaning and relationships. Pedro Antonio and Matilda embody the important Catholic ethic that emphasizes *being* rather than *having*—trusting in God's will and treating others well rather than accumulating wealth. But collective agricultural principles gave way as employers treated labor outside the household unit as a commodity to be bought or sold. As a result, production has become increasingly secularized and is conceived of as a human activity rather than a tangible means of invoking God's material blessing (Briggs, 1981).[10]

Assimilation into a capitalist economy is altering the four cornerstones of life in Norteño—land, language, faith, and family. Land remains a cornerstone of village culture, but the patterns of rural living have changed with the shift from subsistence-seasonal employment to full-time employment. This shift has diminished the practice of mutual assistance by which the tasks of farming life were accomplished. The bonds of neighborliness and community participation—formerly expressed through shared efforts to utilize the land—have grown weaker (Arensberg & Kimball, 1965/1972).[11]

Few in Norteño would disparage the ease of modern life that has come of late to their community. However, tangible gains may cause intangible losses. The different institutions within a community

> help to form the inner life of individual citizens—their imaginations, aims, desires, and fears. These institutions inculcate habits, good and bad.... Because the habits of the heart are learned in childhood ... each generation lives off the spiritual capital of its inheritance, and may not even notice when it is squandering this treasure.... A generation may not grasp until too late the full implications of altering the traditions of the past. (Novak, 1993, p. 196)

The breakdown of communalism as a way of life undermines the intimate interactions among community members. The decreasing communication between the generations is changing how the habits of the heart are learned in childhood. As these attitudes and habits of the past change, the footholds of social support weaken. Samuel Anaya understands, though perhaps not in these terms, that spiritual capital feeds social capital; economic capital threatens both. He laments that social life today is determined more by buying diversions than by participating in community activities.

---

[10]Charles Briggs' doctoral fieldwork in Quemado, New Mexico, looked at how social relations changed with the shift from subsistence agriculture to wage labor.

[11]In *Culture and Community*, Conrad Arensberg and Solon Kimball (1972) explained changes in rural life using four interdependencies: sentiment systems, relational structures, motivations, and objectives.

The depth of unity in the community once came from the repeated rhythms of farming and church practices. Religion is less important for the young. The closing of the parochial school in Norteño left a void of religious teaching, and the priest worries that the children no longer know Scripture. Now, other influences compete for their hearts and minds; less spirituality and prayer guide their lives. Formal education disrupts cultural continuity by offering alternative explanations to the religious ones that guide the lives of older Norteños. Age and denomination divide. The early Sunday mass in Spanish attracts the elderly; the later mass in English draws more young people. And the increasing number of non-Catholics affects the form and content of school and community events.

Community members of the grandparents' generation seem more Spanish than American, the grandchildren more American than Spanish; the parents a cultural bridge spanning two generations and two identities. The Spanish language embodies God's presence in farewells such as *Vaya con Dios*—Go with God. Added to the end of sentences, *si Dios quiere*—God willing—reminds Norteños that only God's will controls their lives. As young people pursue English as their first language, they lose expressions of spirituality that molded the character of their elders.

A less obvious loss is the Spanish vocabulary associated with the agrarian lifestyle. Hispano ethnoscience, the detailed knowledge of nature acquired by spending a lifetime in the outdoors, is being replaced by textbook knowledge. Traditional, mostly unrecorded knowledge about the environment is vanishing as Norteño's linguistic heritage disintegrates.[12] This fragmentation of culture accelerates with the exponential increase in textbook knowledge, thereby posing a paradox: "The advancement of learning ... has in our own day become the fragmentation of learning as well" (McFarland, 1987, p. 5).

The barrier between grandparents and their grandchildren is not just one of language. Lifestyles have changed so dramatically that the cultural lessons and answers for the elders do not always fit the cultural experiences and questions of the young. Vanishing with Spanish is the art of *platicando*—using proverbs, riddles, songs, hymns, legends, ballads, and folktales to pass on wisdom, popular knowledge, and moral precepts from one generation to the next. These forms of communication used to occur in the fields, around the hearth, or at festive occasions (Briggs,

---

[12]Jared Diamond (1994), an evolutionary biologist, has lamented the loss of ecological knowledge associated with the decreasing linguistic diversity in the world. Munro S. Edmonson (1957) talked about the vanishing folk theories about nature in *Los Manitos: A Study of Institutional Values*.

1981).[13] Now scary stories from the past of spirits, miracles, and bewitchment appear unreal and superstitious to teenagers who have never experienced such things or have different explanations for what happens to them. Social interaction no longer includes much storytelling. Without stories, the contours of traditional culture lose definition.

Many old Hispano tales are of the righteous and charitable acts of saints; of popular beliefs about rural living—getting a hen to lay eggs, locating a site to dig a well; of magical views of the past. The role of storytelling is shifting from transmitting cultural knowledge to safeguarding heritage and ethnicity, because oral traditions take on a different meaning in text. Preservation by the written word reduces the relevance and embellishment that come with retelling stories in particular situations to appropriate audiences. This diminished role of stories in everyday life threatens the extent and vitality of Spanish tradition in Northern New Mexico.[14]

To speak of losses is to risk romanticizing the past and underestimating the gains of the present. Education has rechanneled cultural talents toward the mainstream. Young people like Julie Anaya have more opportunities for postsecondary education and careers. Exposure, abundance, convenience, tolerance, choice, equity—all compose the circumstances of modern adolescence. Families no longer work the land as much together, but fewer men have to leave their families in search of seasonal employment for survival. The role of women has expanded outside the home. Having broken out of their centuries-old cultural boundaries, Norteños take pride in their ability to compete with Anglos for academic and athletic recognition, for educational opportunities, for jobs and status.

The changing cornerstones of the Anaya family depict how economic, religious, and other demographic influences are indeed shifting the community identity. As the form of the community changes, the pattern of the culture changes. Life histories highlight forces of change at work in

---

[13]Charles Briggs (1981) described *platicando* as pedagogically oriented conversations about the past. He conducted doctoral fieldwork in Quemado, New Mexico, about the history of Hispano society from 1750 to 1929. He wrote about the changing modes of holding and exploiting land resources and about the principles that underlie social relations and how Hispanos talk about the past.

[14]Some favorite publications of Hispano stories and proverbs include Aurelio M. Espinosa (1985), *The Folklore of Spain in the American Southwest: Traditional Spanish Folk Literature in Northern New Mexico and Southern Colorado*; José Griego y Maestas and Rudolfo A. Anaya (1980), *Cuentos: Tales from the Hispanic Southwest*; Paulette Atencio and Rubén Cobos (1991), *Cuentos from My Childhood: Legends and Folktales of Northern New Mexico*; Sabine R. Ulibarri (1993), *Tierra Amarilla: Stories of New Mexico/Cuentos de Nuevo Mexico*; Rubén Cobos (1985), *Refranes: Southwestern Spanish Proverbs*.

Norteño. These forces intersect with individual biographies and create turning points and adaptations. The relationship between self and past, whether developed in school or embedded in community life, can be reclaimed by challenging all that has been remembered or not remembered for us. How students construct their own narratives about their roots depends on what they discover and recover from others' narratives, and on which narratives are missing (Courts, 1997; Hall, 1991).

5

Domains of Individuality:
Public and Private

[T]here are two ways a person is individualized.... [W]hile one suffers a diminished sense of *private* individuality by becoming assimilated into public society, such assimilation makes possible the achievement of *public* individuality.

—Rodriguez (1982, p. 26)

As the shape of culture changes, the inward and outward pulls create a tension between, as well as within, the generations. Some Norteños fear the centrifugal force of the public domain—everything authoritative that occurs outside the community. They question whether the achievements of public individuality need to develop at the expense of private individuality—everything familial and intimate that occurs within the community.[1]

My research began with looking at who Norteño students are learning to be. In evaluating the many messages they receive from family, friends, educators, and the outside world, I discovered the community's concern about who the students are *not* learning to be. There is a fundamental disagreement in Norteño about developing public and private individuality; this became clear to me as I observed how teachers prepare rural Hispano youth for living in dual cultural worlds. Norteño's teachers design curricula based on what they believe these students need to understand about themselves and the outside world before going out into it.

---

[1]In his controversial memoir, *Hunger of Memory*, Richard Rodriguez (1982) developed the terms *public individuality* and *private individuality* to analyze how education altered his life as a Mexican immigrant in the United States. He argued against pluralism, claiming that advantage for the socially disadvantaged does not rise out of difference, but rather out of conformity.

In this chapter, I combine observations and interviews to present classroom snapshots that illustrate how six Norteño educators influence the
way students develop their own domains of individuality. These six differ
in their insider–outsider status, ethnicity, gender, religion, and length of
employment in the Norteño School District. In the particular moments
depicted, some teachers emphasize developing private individuality that
is attached to the community; others stress public individuality linked to
the Anglo world; others express ambivalence about the gains and losses
associated with both approaches. All want their students to receive a rigorous, first-rate education that enables upward mobility.

LUISA: THE WE OF ME

Reaching my teens, the stories of my parents' past grew distant and less
important as I became more and more Anglicized. And in my twenties, I
reached the point where, regrettably, I didn't want to hear about our past
because I couldn't really believe in my parents' stories anymore.

Then, turning thirty and finding the woman that I wished to marry and
have my children with, I suddenly realized how empty I'd feel if I couldn't
tell my own children about our ancestral roots.

—Villaseñor (1991, p. xi)

Luisa reads the above passage from Victor Villaseñor's *Rain of Gold* to
seniors in her Advanced Writing class. She tells them that her past, too,
became less important as she became more Anglicized. She is preparing
to explain the origins of an oral history assignment that requires each
student to do 5 hours of interviewing with an elderly relative, transcribe
the interviews, and write a final narrative that weaves the stories and
personality of the elder relative with old photos and documents. Luisa,
who grew up in a neighboring village, wants her students to discover
"the we of me"—how their lives are connected to those of others. As
Luisa expresses her objectives for the project, one can hear her own sense
of nostalgia and urgency:

This project came from a feeling in the community that their history and
your history are being lost because people aren't asking questions anymore. These stories you are hearing will mean more to you when you're
older and only have the stories left to remind you of your ancestors. Maybe
you'll be even closer to your families after doing this project, and maybe
you'll speak more Spanish.

After the first round of interviews, students complain of running out of things to talk about. She cautions those who found some of the stories unreal not to underestimate the importance of spirituality to the elders as a way of explaining the world around them. She reads them another passage from *Rain of Gold*:

> Some of the things that my parents and relatives told me were just too foreign, too fantastic, for my modern mind to accept.... I grew to doubt all their stories.... [L]ittle by little, I began to see that maybe one person's reality was, indeed, another's fantasy—especially if their childhood perceptions of the world were so different. I came to understand why my father had always told me that it was easy to call another's religion superstitious. (Villaseñor 1991, p. xii)

Luisa thumbs through books with photos from the old days to give students ideas about lifestyle issues they could ask about. She urges the students to ask the *ancianos* to describe a typical day from morning to evening. What did they do for fun? Did they buy goods in the store? What was their wedding like? Stopping at a page showing two boys hauling water from the river during winter, Luisa reminisces.

> We didn't have indoor plumbing and running water. We were so poor that we used to get only two pairs of shoes each year, one for the summer and one at Christmastime. In between we had to put cardboard in our shoes if they had holes. We called shoes with holes "blow outs."

Such a lifestyle stands in stark contrast to the modern home this fashionable teacher lives in now. Using personal anecdotes, Luisa portrays for the students a way of growing up that is very different from their own. She tells them about her grandmother's last will and testament that listed these worldly possessions: three mattresses, sheets, and eight American dollars. She describes how large families used to live in small houses, spreading mattresses out on the floor at night and piling them with the blankets in the morning. She shares her relatives' stories:

> My grandmother can still vividly recall the day grandfather came with his padrino to ask my great-grandfather for her hand in marriage. A guy couldn't just say, "I want to marry you." He had to take his godfather to ask on his behalf, and the woman's family could say no.

> My great-grandfather was extremely strict. He had never allowed any of his children to date. They didn't allow dating. My parents told me that my

father tried to follow my mother when she rode horseback to go find strawberries to pick, and my mother would wave to him behind her back. To
keep her sister from telling their parents, my mother would pick her sister's share of the strawberries.

Few students recall hearing many *cuentos*; the occasions when people
would tell stories are no longer part of the daily routine. Stories were not
told for their own sake. They were told to make a point or to serve some
social purpose. Luisa affirms this when she recalls the role of stories in
her life:

> Adults would use *cuentos* to keep our minds preoccupied while we were do-
> ing hard work. Women would tell *chistes*—jokes—while embroidering.
> With their eyes down, they would say a lot that they might not say if they
> were looking each other in the eye.

While sorting fragile family land documents in class and showing students how to use such documents for research, Luisa talks about the land:

> My family used to be the largest landholders in the village. These are the
> documents where my great-great-grandmother passed the property to my
> great-grandfather. Now the responsibility for caring for the land has fallen
> on me, and I can't handle everyone's property. Some are thinking of selling
> in order to have enough money to buy a house in California. I'm the only
> one interested in buying it to keep it in the family, but I don't know if we
> can afford it.

A female student replies, "My father told me to never sell the land. It's all
we have." I ask Luisa if she thinks her two daughters will stay in Norteño
to live. She answers, "My youngest, yes, she loves it here, but my teen-
ager says she wants to go to the city."

Luisa's father recently passed away, so the tradition of passing on the
land is of immediate concern. To illustrate to students how the best writing comes from personal experience, Luisa wrote this paragraph about
her father and the meaning of the land in his life:

> We buried my dad today in a piece of land we never owned and we never
> worked. Strange. Stranger yet is the fact that he requested it before he died.
> Still, my tears are hard to stop when I think of this great man of *la tierra* [the
> earth], of *el terreno santo y bendito* [sacred and blessed soil], being buried in
> a plot of earth which was not familiar to him. For 76 years he worked his own

land with his hands, with picks and shovels, with horses, with plows, with tractors. The land was his, not because he had inherited it, but because his labor and his sweat had claimed it. The labor and sweat of at least eight generations of Tafoyas is mingled with my dad's in what he always referred to as, *la tierra de mi gente* [the land of my people].

Students face several challenges in conducting their interviews: the language barrier, resistance to being tape-recorded, a strong sense of privacy, a reluctance to remember the past. Luisa asks the students to evaluate the interview experience:

> **Luisa:** How did you feel about the connections between previous generations and yourself?
>
> **Martín:** I want to pass on what I've learned to my children. I guess my fear is that I don't want to get forgotten when I'm dead in the earth, so I don't want to forget my relatives. Besides, we need to learn from their mistakes.
>
> **Luisa:** If nothing else, it's showed us the importance of keeping records. If we don't care about those traditions because we don't understand why they were important, we don't have a connection with our families. Did anyone become closer? Did you grow in your relationship? Do you understand them better as people?
>
> **Cathy:** My reality and my grandmother's are too different.
>
> **Ken:** I told my grandpa I want to know more than just what he wanted to tell me for the class assignment, so he told me things off the record.
>
> **Luisa:** If you learn from your family, you end up understanding more about why you are the way you are.

The purpose of the assignment is to give students a sense of their own history, be it Anglo, Indian, or Hispanic, and to develop their skills in interviewing, researching, and synthesizing information. This writing class allows Luisa to explore her own identity as her students explore theirs, but the other subjects she teaches are primarily vocational. In those subject areas, change is exponential and universal: "In my business education classes, the most important culture I can share with all students is the culture of technology." Luisa would not characterize herself as one who advocates remaining. She encourages her students to become all they can. Knowing and recording who they have been is part of coming to terms with their heritage—going back to find their own beginning.

GEORGEANN: THE LINKS OF COMMON KNOWLEDGE

In Georgeann's social studies classroom, a red banner stretches fully across the front of her desk—"The Power of Knowledge." Bulletin boards display the Declaration of Independence, the Emancipation Proclamation, and pictures of significant African American leaders. Up above the blackboard hangs a poster of the diverse faces of our nation's people—red, black, white, yellow, brown. The profiles of the faces fit together in the shape of the United States above the slogan "Attitude Is Everything." A smaller sign says, "Things Do Not Change. We Change."

Georgeann is an Anglo, an outsider who came to the Southwest in the 1950s and to the Norteño School District in 1990. During her many summer travels, Georgeann picks up lots of stories to tell her students. Last summer she traveled 60 days, visited 39 national parks and historical sites, and logged 8,270 miles. Her weekly class schedule includes daily discussions about current events and geography.

As they enter the classroom each day, students are expected to write some fact about current events on the blackboard. Georgeann adds to their facts a list of names, such as Yitzhak Rabin, Cesar Chavez, Spike Lee, Boris Yeltsin, Manuel Noriega, Ice Man. "Who are these people who have been in the news lately?" Only a few students appear informed, so pooling knowledge prepares them for their biweekly current events quiz.

Fridays are devoted to reading aloud from a classroom set of *Current Events*, a weekly publication with world news and articles directed at teenagers. Why devote so much time to current events and geography? Georgeann explains:

> To me, you just can't get out in the world without knowing what's going on out there, whether you're going to college or to the workforce. Some of these students don't have televisions and don't get the news. Few families subscribe to newspapers or magazines, and the majority of the students don't read much. They can't visualize what part of a map to look at for different countries. They don't have the common knowledge about how things happen that we all take for granted. When I make references to landmark events, books, ideas, people, or places, these students often don't know what I'm talking about.

On her own initiative, Georgeann created a team to participate in a geography and current events competition for New Mexico's Rural Education Consortium. Competing with seven rural schools, Norteño's team came home with first place.

Georgeann uses every opportunity to broaden the students' horizons and to expose them to what is common knowledge in the world outside Norteño. Maps are everywhere for quick reference. Pulling down one to show the route of the ongoing Iditarod dogsled race between Anchorage and Nome, she speaks to her juniors about Alaska:

"Seward's Icebox" is the nickname for Alaska, which was purchased for 2 cents per acre. Alaska is the Aleut word for "great land," and Chief Seattle controlled Alaska in the early days until his power was taken away from him.

What's the capital of Alaska? Juneau. If you see a word with 'eau,' it's usually French. That's one way we can tell where the French traders went.

Georgeann's definition of bilingual education includes teaching what foreign words used in English mean. Then she makes a pitch for students to go to Alaska:

As much as you love New Mexico, you can make good money up there in just a few years. There's phenomenal fishing and good hunting for those of you who like that.

Lecturing about a land grant made by Mexico to start a colony of Americans in Texas, Georgeann offers an interpretation closer to how Norteños experienced American settlement:

Georgeann: Where did American colonists come from to Texas? The cotton states. Do you think those Americans became Catholics?

Students: No.

Georgeann: Spoke Spanish?

Students: No.

Georgeann: Many Americans moved there because of the free land, cheap living, and eventually the Americans outnumbered the Mexicans in Texas. The Mexican government tried to control the colonists and discourage others from coming. Do you think the Anglos stopped coming to Texas?

Students: No.

Georgeann: Americans were like the illegal immigrants today, crossing the river illegally. What do you think the Anglos were doing?

    Students: Stealing land.
   Georgeann: In 1836, Texas won its independence—the Lone Star
               Republic—bringing in a period of ethnic intolerance.
               There's lots of prejudice against Mexicans, Catholics,
               Blacks, Hispanics, Indians. Texas even passed laws that
               said Indians couldn't live in the state. The famous
               Texas Rangers were set up to protect Anglos. They
               weren't as bad as the KKK, but bad enough.

Georgeann's lectures are full of facts, delivered with humor. She personalizes current events, either by relating what is happening elsewhere to what is happening in New Mexico or by using an anecdote from her life to illustrate a point. With cross-cultural sensitivity, Georgeann exposes students to the outside world while connecting history lessons to their lives and helping them develop a strong sense of their place in history.

In spite of her teaching excellence, Georgeann's future in Norteño depends on her earning bilingual certification. To Georgeann, bilingual education does not mean just speaking Spanish in class. Georgeann's curricular orientation exemplifies her working definition of bilingual education: teaching a culturally appropriate curriculum that amplifies ethnic history rather than treating it as compensatory. Her approach validates students' private individuality by linking their understanding of their unique history with essential common knowledge that will allow them to be successful in the public arena.

ALFONSO: *LA IMPORTANCIA DE SABER DOS IDIOMAS* [THE IMPORTANCE OF KNOWING TWO LANGUAGES]

[W]ords are alive and carry our history, our thoughts, our feelings, and they unite us. They are the total memory of a culture.
              —Mondragón and Roybal (1994, p. 6)

Alfonso singles out this statement in the premier issue of the regional publication *La Herencia del Norte: Our Past, Our Present, Our Future.* A Norteño native who serves as the elementary school bilingual director, he worries about the rapid loss of the local language and traditional way of life. He believes culture and identity are embedded in language. When a community abandons its language, it loses a part of its being.

The bilingual program tries to enrich the cultural awareness and self-esteem of children through classroom projects and parental involvement. The *Padres, Niños y La Escuela* newsletter from the Norteño Elementary School Bilingual Office goes out each month to parents. Alfonso writes passionately to the parents about *la belleza de nuestra cultura*, the beauty of our culture, telling them the children have to know where they came from to know where they are going:

> *Cuando una persona se cría dentro de una cultura, aprende a apreciar de donde viene y para donde va. La cultura hispana e india es muy rica, llena de tradiciones y costumbres lindas que ninguna otra raza tiene.... Como padres debemos enseñar esta belleza a los niños.* [When one is raised in a culture, one learns to appreciate where one is from and where one is going. The Indo-Hispanic culture is very rich, full of traditions and wonderful customs that no other people have. As parents, we must teach this beauty to the children.]

Paperwork can wait. Alfonso prefers to visit classes. When he greets third graders in Spanish, they answer loudly and in unison, *"Buenas tardes."* Strumming his guitar, Alfonso teaches children the state song: *"Así es Nuevo Méjico, esta tierra del sol, con los cerros y valles, flores y frutales, Así es Nuevo Méjico"* [This is New Mexico, land of sun, with foothills and valleys, flowers and fruits, this is New Mexico].[2]

Alfonso speaks to the children slowly and clearly in Spanish, without translating to English:

> *Ustedes con un nombre español tienen que aprender el español, porque algún día se vaya a Santa Fe y se le pregunte, "¿Usted habla español?" Si tiene que decir "No," qué vergüenza que no sabe el idioma de su nombre.* [Those of you with Spanish names need to learn Spanish, because someday you may go to Santa Fe and be asked, "Do you speak Spanish?" If you have to say "No," you'll be embarrassed because you don't know the language that goes with your name.]

Alfonso holds today's parents responsible for the loss of Spanish in the home even though the schools restricted his generation from speaking Spanish. When he attended Norteño's parochial school, students who overheard other kids speaking Spanish would go tell the nuns and get the other kids sent to the principal's office. Alfonso, whose family spoke only Spanish at home, was in the principal's office a lot. Language separated the worlds of home and school. Now that the Spanish language restriction at school no longer exists, the home language for three quarters

---

[2]*Así es Nuevo Méjico* was adopted as the state song in 1971. Amadeo Lucero, a retired teacher who taught in rural New Mexican villages, composed the song.

of the children is English. To Alfonso, a person is less Hispanic if he or she does not speak Spanish:

> *Es muy importante para nuestros hijos que aprendan su lengua nativa bien y también el inglés. No hay causa más rica que saber dos lenguas.... Es vergüenza cuando uno encuentra a un Hispano que no puede comunicar en su propia lengua.* [It's very important that our children learn their native language well and also English. There is no richer cause than knowing two languages. It is a shame when one meets Hispanos who cannot communicate in their own language.]

Alfonso feels embarrassed to speak English to someone who is Hispanic. On the bookshelf next to Alfonso's desk is a stack of children's standard Spanish books that he is considering translating into "our Spanish," the colloquial dialect. Thumbing through the *Hispanic* monthly magazine, he notes, "It's so refreshing to see good images of Hispanics. The news and movies are always showing us as being bad." Around the office stand models of a *molino* for grinding wheat, a hacienda with *ristras de chili* [hanging red chili strands], *La Sembrita de Mi Abuelo* [the figure of an old man planting his field with a horse-drawn plow], *una era* [goats walking on a mound to separate the wheat from the chaff], *un horno* for baking bread, and replicas of churches from Northern New Mexico. Alfonso and the principal sent a memo to parents, encouraging them to work on such cultural projects with their children:

> It is important that our children maintain their culture. We would like to extend an invitation for you and your child to get involved in developing a cultural project which we or our ancestors used.... This is a part of history which our children must familiarize themselves with in order for them to develop as a whole.

Alfonso believes adamantly that there cannot be just one culture in the United States, even if everyone speaks the same language. He illustrates his point with a story:

> There was a pig on a farm, and the owners, who had little knowledge about the nature of pigs, used to wash him every day to try to change his identity. They wanted him as a pet, a clean pet. But that's not the nature of a pig, so they were trying to change his culture.

Alfonso believes that Hispano identity and language are intrinsic and cannot be changed by imitation of Anglo ways. The values dear to Alfonso—God's presence, knowledge of the land, a strong sense of community, the stories and songs of the past—stem from his cultural and linguistic heritage. The depth of Alfonso's feelings comes from his faith as a *Penitente* —Brother of Penance—in the *morada* next to the school. The Penitentes' *alabados* [hymns] and rituals are conducted only in Spanish. Alfonso moves with ease across cultural boundaries, learning from the Anglo world without forgetting that his identity is rooted in the Norteño world.

KATE: WHERE ETHNIC PRIDE ENDS AND PREJUDICE BEGINS

Kate's passion is to teach people how to write. She believes that writing empowers people. Her philosophy is to start from the students' personal experiences, designing assignments that allow them to express what they do and feel:

> I used to be the only Chicana in the English department at Northern New Mexico Community College. Those New Yorkers on the faculty would have the Hispano students write about global issues rather than about the land, the acequias, who they are, what they do. Most of these Hispanos are going to stay here and need to know who they are.

> Writing is the key to everything. If you can take whatever information you have and write about it, you've internalized it. It rolls around in your head several times before it comes out of your hand, into the pen, and onto the paper.

> Writing can help us deal with some of the pain of life. Just yesterday I gave an assignment to write a poem with every line beginning with "Someday …" This one girl wrote, "Someday my dad will stop drinking. Someday my parents will stop fighting."

Kate's ancestors built the plaza for an Hispano village about 25 miles away from Norteño. Many of her family members attended Protestant mission schools and converted. Her parents and Anglo husband have taken her to other places—Maryland, Hawaii, New Hampshire. By living away from her culture, she has learned about its treasures. A relative newcomer to the Norteño School District, Kate serves as a bilingual coordinator. Her messages to her students address the complexity of living in dual cultural worlds, and she tries to help her students see beyond Norteño.

Kate's eighth graders are working on a unit called "A World of Difference," a curriculum about prejudice awareness published by *The New Mexican* newspaper. Kate worries about the intolerance and ridicule some Norteño students face. Her own half-Anglo children are labeled "hippies" if they dress differently. Her children and other Anglos have come home from school in tears, wanting to dye their hair black and change the color of their eyes in order to fit in with the Hispano majority.

Kate's students have already completed a variety of exercises and projects leading up to today's discussion about generalizing and stereotyping. They looked at themselves, their attitudes, beliefs, likes, dislikes, family tree. They wrote essays (entitled "What Happened to Derek Smith?") about an Anglo student who was essentially driven out of the school by prejudice. Out of a class of 19 students, 16 are Hispano, 2 Anglo, and 1 Indian. Kate starts off by telling the students a story about when she stereotyped people:

Kate: When I attended Santa Fe High School, I remember the stereotyping regarding "stompers"—those who wore cowboy boots. The students were grouped as stompers, smokers, jocks, et cetera. I recall playing the game of jacks with my girlfriends and excluding others by saying, "Tick, tock, the game is locked." I hope that girl we wouldn't let play survived our torture. I think school shouldn't be a place of pain. It's like going to the torture chamber for some kids.

In almost every situation in life, we're confronted with stereotypes. That's life. We group people by religion, race. I don't like that.

What does prejudice mean? It comes from prejudging. What does judging mean? Making decisions. What's a generalization?

Marty: A definition that refers to a whole group.

Kate: Have you ever heard the Spanish expression, *"Díme con quien andas y te diré quien eres"*—Tell me who you hang around with, and I'll tell you about yourself—or the saying, "If you lie with a dog with fleas, you'll get fleas"? What's the difference between disliking or being prejudiced against someone?

Carlos: Dislike means you don't like someone because of their personality. Prejudice means you don't like them because of their nationality.

Kevin (Anglo): Prejudice means you don't like them because of their race. Dislike means you don't like them because they're mean to someone else.

Kate: Dislike comes from personal experience. Prejudice comes from not liking because of something you've never experienced.

The students read role plays regarding disliking and being prejudiced to distinguish between the two. Then Kate asks them to give her examples of prejudices and of dislikes.

Melissa: A person who says he doesn't like to play with Indians is prejudiced.

James: I have an example for you. Some people don't like you, Mrs. Thompson, because they say you're prejudiced.

Kate: What am I prejudiced against?

James: They say you protect a certain group of people.

Kate: What do you think of that? [The students shrug.] *Um ... I think I'm proud of that protection.*

After class, Kate and I discuss the student's comment about her being prejudiced.

Kate: Isn't it ironic that by promoting tolerance, I'm viewed as prejudiced! Even though I'm married to a *güero* [Anglo outsider], I'm a Chicana through and through. I have struggled with the double-edged sword of education and acculturation in the white man's world. I think we're going in reverse. I sometimes have second thoughts about the bilingual program. Maybe by emphasizing the preservation of our culture, we're causing a backlash against the other. Maybe we shouldn't teach culture in school and should just let culture take its course, letting what's intrinsically important to people about the culture be what survives. Culture is only meaningful if taught in the home as part of daily living. Let's preserve what we can—the goodness—and not be against the outsiders.

The dynamics of race and ethnicity in Norteño life are contrary to the majority–minority dynamics in American life. Kate faces the dilemma of teaching students who are a minority nationally, but are the majority locally. "How do I instill in these students a sense of pride and a knowledge of who they are without creating intolerance? I want them to be open to all people of all cultures. How do I prepare these students to go outside Norteño where *they* will be the minority?"

HECTOR: LEAVE TO MAKE SOMETHING OF YOURSELF

Hector stands out in the hall between classes, greeting kids with a smile, a handshake, or a hug. An Hispanic raised south of Albuquerque and married to a local, he knows students by name and family background and watches their faces to know how things are going. When Hector speaks to me, I hear the voice of one who has walked in his students' shoes:

Here we have the really sharp kids or the poorly motivated kids, with no middle ground. I need to push a "you can" message rather than just coddle the students. The spirit is within us. Just hang in there, and then your life is your own. The bottom line is we can wallow in our sorrows, but the spirit is within us to go beyond. If we're going to go beyond, we need to emerge as leaders. We've got to fight. That's why God put us on earth. All He's asking is for us to keep pushing forward. Don't let your spirit die. Once you give up, you die. As long as you continue to struggle, you continue to live. You've got to look for the positive.

I got my "shoot for the moon" philosophy from my younger brother, who told me he was aiming for the Olympics. He figured that every winner came from someplace and was the child of someone, so why not him, an Hispanic from a small town in New Mexico? My brother got an athletic scholarship to college, was named most valuable team member every year, and became a doctor.

A few weeks into the school year, Hector makes the rounds to talk to all the ninth graders. As he enters the classroom, the boys take off their hats. Hector commands student respect through his expectations for the students and his role as basketball coach and counselor. Hector pulls over a chair and puts one leg on it, leaning toward the students with his elbow on his knee:

Hector: Now that you're freshmen, the buck stops here. Everything from now on is on your record. You're going to pay for everything you do. How many of you are planning to graduate from high school? [Most of the students raise their hands.] From college? [Half raise their hands.] Go to the military? [Three raise their hands.] Go to a trade school? [A few raise their hands.]

When I was your age, we only had two choices: Go to jail or go to the services. Now things have changed. The military is no longer a place for high school dropouts to go. Because there are more high-tech jobs in the service, you can't get into the military without a high school diploma.

Roberto, let's think about you 10 years down the road—25 years old with a wife and kids. What do you think it would take financially to make it? Own a house?

Have a vehicle? Take a vacation once a year? I'd at least hope you'd have those things in your life.

Roberto: $35,000 to $36,000?

Hector: Let's add $10,000 to make $46,000. You could always be struggling. I hope you want something good for yourself to be comfortable. What kind of job could you do today that would earn that kind of money?

Roberto: Electrical engineering, medicine.

Hector: You could look at different things. Let me give you an example. I have 13 years in education—about halfway through my career. I came in at mid-$30,000. I have a brother who's finishing his internship as an anesthesiologist. How much do you think he'll make? He's looking at $170- to $180,000 starting salary per year. You want to look at what makes you happy as an individual. If you want things, you need to find a way to earn that kind of money. Educators are resigned to living with simple things.

You need to think of some career. I'm not saying you have to become a lawyer, doctor, or engineer. Other professional trades are worthwhile, but there's got to be something beyond high school! You're going to need a certified license if you choose a trade. I'm sure you all know someone who is a great carpenter or auto mechanic. Thing is, they don't make much money. Why?

Patty: They didn't graduate.

Hector: They're always working for someone else, because they haven't gone the extra yard to get their license. The contractor who has the license pays these guys $6 to $7 per hour, but he makes the money because he has the license. You need to start thinking about something beyond high school if you want to make it. Be the person in charge! Working at McDonald's or cutting hair doesn't cut it. You're too good to just flip hamburgers. You need to think of yourself as being the person on top. First thing you have to do is graduate from high school.

What would be the major problem continuing education after high school?

Aaron: Money.

Hector: How are you going to get the money?

Aaron: Go to work.

Hector: You'll rent a place to live, get a car, get a job, get a little cash in your pocket, and soon you'll lose interest in going to school, or you won't be able to afford to pay tuition because of the rent, food costs, and car payments. That's what happens the majority of the time, so it's best to go straight to school. How can you do it?

Patty: Financial aid.

Hector: Who gives it? State and federal governments. There's one good time to be poor in your life, from a family that doesn't have much money—your senior year in high school. If you have decent grades—I didn't say great—and come from a family with less than $20,000 a year, you can pretty much get your education paid for at a college or trade school.

José: What if you want to go out of state?

Hector: It's prorated. Let's say you want to go to Notre Dame. It would cost about $20,000 per year. Let's say you would qualify for a grant covering 80% of the cost, regardless of the cost. They would pay $16,000. There are other options—student loans. Some of you may not want to take out a loan, but let's figure it out. If you borrow $5,000 each year while attending Notre Dame, you owe $20,000. Is that worth it for what you're getting? So many of you wouldn't hesitate to borrow $20,000 to get a new car. You could start in working for someone else and not borrow, or you could borrow and have a better starting point a few years later. But you've got to do something after high school—trade school, the military, or college. You're not going to get what you want if you sit back and let the chips fall where they do. You need to be aggressive and get what you want.

Moving down the hall, Hector pushes a TV-VCR cart into Mrs. Thompson's room. Teachers have been complaining about the poor academic progress of the seventh graders. When Hector asks "How many of you will graduate from high school?" all the seventh graders predict they will. They are startled by the school's drop-out rate—25% might not graduate. After showing the students the video *Staying in School*, Hector leans against the wall and makes his pitch:

Hector: Look around this classroom. If the trend stays the same, five of you in this class will not graduate. That hits close to home. That's the trend. I've been here 7 years. People like you always say you're going to graduate, but what causes some not to?

Bennie: Laziness.

Hector: What kind of laziness?

Bennie: Students don't do their homework.

Hector: Mrs. Thompson, do all these students do their homework?

Mrs. Thompson: No, I just sent out semester notices because of incomplete work.

Hector: You'd better get some study skills. You'd better turn in your homework, or you won't pass. Mrs. Thompson, do these kids study for tests?

Mrs. Thompson: No.

Hector: Did you lie to me? You all said you're going to graduate, but you're not doing what it takes. Why don't you?

Shirley: TV.

Hector: You've got to understand that we were not all born equal. We were born alone; we die alone. I know some of you come from families with alcohol and drug problems, parents who don't care, parents who are on welfare. But you are capable of making it through if you take the initiative. There's a test you have to pass in 10th grade. There's no way to cheat on it. Same for getting into college. You have to learn this information. There's no "smart pill." There's no way you can learn to write well without doing it; read well without doing it. You have to go through the process. You must study. You must read books. You must go to class. You've got to start preparing for what you want to be right now. You have to be disciplined and get your homework done. Once you get yourself trained to do those things, it'll become natural.

Mrs. Thompson: One of the reasons people drop out of school is because they don't feel good about themselves. What happens is that when you don't come with your work, you feel embarrassed. You hate me for giving you homework. Then you get the notice and have to try to hide it from your parents. The F comes, and you can't wait until you're 16 for your problems with school to be over. Get your work in every day, rather than slouching down in your seat and hoping I won't call on you. You can make yourself feel good or bad. It's up to you now. Avoid the staircase spiral that goes down instead of up.

Hector: It doesn't just happen. Learning is a process. You see people on welfare who don't work, who get money and are living better than people who work hard every day. You've got to understand that government benefits are being cut. I think by the time you're young adults, there won't be any welfare or social security benefits. We're living too well in this country. If you're not making it in this country, you get taken care of. By the time you guys get out of school, there won't be programs out there. If you have in mind that someone's going to take care of you, forget it. You can either take care of yourself or steal.

Mrs. Thompson: Consider a life on welfare. I have a friend who receives $250 per month. His rent is $175 per month, which leaves him with $75 for him and his daughter. He receives some food stamps. He pays utility bills—just enough to keep from getting them turned off. He can't buy clothes for his daughter. He can't take her to McDonald's. He's dependent on others. He has to sell things just to buy some gas. It's a terrible life to be on welfare.

Hector: If you don't take advantage of your education, it'll come back to haunt you. If you've been a bad student, there's time to change. For a good student, there's always a way to get a college education. If there's one thing I want you to understand, it's that there's time to change, but you have to make the change. You make choices every day. Your choice about your education will determine your future.

What makes an A/B student different from a D/F student? Self-discipline, which leads to self-confidence. You've got to want to make something out of yourselves. You've got to want to be somebody.

Hector creates a stark picture of what these students are up against. He tolerates no excuses for failure or living on the dole. Being an outsider, Hector appreciates what Norteño offers these students, but he knows the potential waiting to be tapped if they go beyond the village limits. Students cross a reminder of this potential daily when they walk over the school's motto written on the entrance doormat—*Aprender Es Avanzar* [To Learn Is to Advance]. Hector's game plan targets students who cannot imagine what a future away from Norteño might be like or how to get there.

BOLÍVAR: STAND AND DELIVER

When I asked high school students to describe a positive classroom experience, everyone mentioned the one teacher who always stands and delivers—Bolívar, a local who recently retired. What does he deliver? Lessons punctuated with a sort of running commentary meant to motivate his students and teach discipline, responsibility, and honesty as well as mathematics.

Bolívar is Norteño's math evangelist, much like Jaime Escalante, the California math teacher whose work is depicted in the movie *Stand and Deliver*. The resemblance is striking, but coincidental. Bolívar did not fashion his teaching style after Escalante's. A student pointed out the similarity and brought the movie for Bolívar to see, and Bolívar began showing the movie to his students to reinforce the messages he wants them to learn about themselves: who they are and who they can become if they work hard. His own life epitomizes "local boy who made good and still remained local." Bolívar never hesitates to share his story with students and to remind them of advantages they should appreciate:

> You students have a beautiful school, wonderful teachers, nice classrooms, lockers, a library, and facilities like a new gym, a weight room, an audiovisual room—things we never dreamed about. I remember we used to run all the way to the parochial school to eat for a dime. There were a lot of us in our family—12 kids. During those times when father was unemployed, it was hard to come up with 70 to 80 cents a day for everyone to eat. I remember a lot of times mother would pass out the dimes in the morning, but I would say I still had money, even if it was not true. I just drank water and that was it.

Bolívar's messages about the outside world draw on the hard times he faced being the first in his family to go to college. When he attended Norteño High School, there was no guidance counselor to caution him, to make suggestions. To pay for college, he washed dishes in the university cafeteria, cleaned rooms and bathrooms as a janitor, and pumped gas until late at night. He started studying when all the others were already done. He lacked the academic preparation expected, and the memories of humiliation still hurt:

> Around the third week, I had to make some kind of a report with footnotes and a bibliography. I turned it in like I used to write my book reports here in Norteño. The teacher just threw it back at me and laughed. I remember her asking me, "Where did you go to school? Don't you know about bibliographies? How to use the library catalog?" No, I had never seen a card catalog since a library was nonexistent in Norteño.

Bolívar almost quit. Only his family's pride in him kept him from joining the army. Wanting other students from Norteño never to suffer from such an inadequate academic background, he returned to Norteño with the resolve to teach students the mathematical concepts they need to know to compete with students from other schools. So what do students need to know about the outside world before leaving Norteño? Bolívar feels strongly about how the school should prepare students:

> Students need to understand it's competitive out there. They have to buckle down. Nobody is going to give them anything. If they're going to have a good chance, the best thing they can get is a good quality education. Without it, they're going to have a strike against them. We should be teaching honors classes in mathematics, in science, in English—you name it. Whoever has a good command of the English language has a better chance of getting that job.

A math teacher is an unlikely hero, but Bolívar is an inspiration to his students nonetheless. His stories, attitude, and approach motivate students. Math Olympics, calculus, engineering career exploration—with these activities, Bolívar pushes his students to compete outside of Norteño and to set high career goals. He wants his students to know that they are just as capable of excelling at a difficult subject like calculus as the most privileged Anglo students are. He believes that any student can learn, as long as the student has *ganas*—the desire.

With strong character and beliefs, Bolívar balances discipline and high expectations with spunk, humor, and caring. He snaps his fingers, calling out a series of numbers for students to calculate in their heads. His fun math contest between boys and girls fosters mental acuity with numbers and a team spirit in the classroom. Students know he is there for them, and they want to please him:

Mary: Bolívar is constantly telling us, "Do it right. It'll pay off later." He is not only our teacher; he counsels us. He doesn't say, "Do this." He puts it in different words. He says, "If you want to be somebody, you want to do this." Rather than putting us down for making mistakes, he encourages us to do better. He always makes you want to learn by giving us reassuring messages like "You're going to succeed in life."

Cristina: Bolívar always tells us not to just put out 100%, but 110%, to make sure we understand what's going on—the process, how we got where we're at. He encouraged me to go on not just in math, but in school too—to do something for myself, to make it out there. Bolívar tells us that in his day you could go out, work hard, and go home with enough money to raise a family. Not meaning to scare us, he lets us know that in our day, we're going to have to get the most education we can. He doesn't want us flipping burgers at McDonald's.

Martín: Bolívar urges us to put this town on the map. Maybe we'll be the one to find a cure for AIDS, but everything's got to come from hard work.

Eloy: Bolívar warns us that there's still a lot of prejudice, and we'll have to work twice as hard. Even though there are civil rights laws, employers will hire someone else just because we're ethnic.

Juan: Bolívar says we have three strikes against us—our name, our color, and our heritage. But if you have your education, who cares about what they say about you. You're smarter than them; you can do your job.

Bolívar's enthusiastic teaching makes students feel important. If someone doesn't understand what's going on, he offers individual help after class, or he stops and goes over the concept until everyone catches on.

Jennifer: Bolívar is the greatest teacher I've ever had. At first I used to mess around in that class, until one day he just pulled me to the side and told me I could do it. All I had to do was pay attention in class, and I could get a good grade. He would tell me to stay after class, come after school, during lunch—anytime he'd help me. So I've been going to his class for help in the mornings before school or for lunch. I have gone from an F to a B, just by him talking to me and showing me that he cares.

The current calculus teacher's own story illustrates Bolívar's tenacious belief in potential:

Mr. Trujillo: I was rebellious and dropped out of Norteño High School my sophomore year. It was only because of Bolívar that I came back and succeeded. He began to work with me one-on-one and to excite me about math. After finally graduating in 1969 and doing construction work in Los Angeles, I decided to go to the University of

New Mexico. Now I teach math and work in Los Alamos
in the summers with computers.

Standing in front of the class, Bolívar represents the past and the future for his students. Growing up on a farm in a large family, he had no
childhood. With his father gone to Montana to work, Bolívar took responsibility for the many decisions that had to be made about irrigating,
taking care of the animals, mending the fences, threshing the wheat. He
arrived at kindergarten with a Big Chief tablet to face a teacher speaking
a language he didn't know. He knows what he wants for his students, but
perhaps the strongest message Bolívar delivers to them at graduation is
about remaining in order to become:

There's a saying in Spanish: "*Cuando hallas tu fortuna, no te olvides tu
cuna.*" When you go out there into the world and you make your fortune,
do not forget your roots. Remember who your parents are and be proud.
They've given you your roots—a hometown, culture, values, faith, and
identity. Rely on your roots to help you with the hard times. Today they
give you a more priceless gift—your wings. With these wings comes responsible decisions. Freedom is not free; success not easy. Dare to dream
your dreams. A journey of a thousand miles starts with the first step. Be
proud of your culture, your people, your town, your school. Be proud of
yourself.

                                    ***

These six educators draw on their own experiences to connect with
students. Their character shapes the structure, tone, and agenda in the
classroom. Their messages entice students to develop certain attitudes,
sensitivities, and perceptions. Each of these educators has a different
view of how the school should foster the public and private individuali-
ties of Norteño students. Together, their words create a strong if ambiguous message for Norteño's students: Learn to become while remaining
true to who you are.

Bolívar repeatedly stresses to students the importance of being proud
of who you are, believing in yourself, working hard, and being competitive. Georgeann broadens students' horizons through exposure to
knowledge that is common outside the community. She helps students
link their region to state, national, and international realities. She cares
about the transferability of knowledge, creating opportunities for students to apply what they know to new situations. Hector pushes stu-

dents to go beyond the village limits in order to get enough education to ensure self-sufficiency. Public individuality requires a capacity to compete for all the advantages of the dominant culture. Social, economic, and political empowerment are the promised rewards of full public individuality. The critical issue for socially disadvantaged students is how to become educationally advantaged enough to accomplish structural assimilation, not just cultural assimilation. Structural assimilation refers to the degree to which ethnic groups gain equal status in the major cliques, organizations, and institutions in our society, and the degree to which they participate in political action, economic life, and civic responsibility. Attaining structural assimilation requires going beyond the security of one's own community (Gordon, 1964).

But teachers like Luisa, Kate, and Alfonso worry about the losses that come with public individuality. Are the students learning something that is worth as much as what they are forgetting? Each teacher would answer this question differently, but all agree on the need for historical and cultural reflection that validates a private individuality of hearth and home, church and community. All recognize the danger of deculturalization: losing an inner cultural spirit that holds a set of values in a coherent whole (Jones, 1993). The experiences and values that guided past generations offer lessons to the young. Luisa, Kate, and Alfonso believe that ethnic maintenance will strengthen rather than marginalize the students of Norteño.

A KALEIDOSCOPE OF NEEDS

When asked to identify needs of students, other Norteño teachers mention reading and life skills—job interviewing, presenting oneself, handling money, searching for a place to live—that contribute to how well students fare in the outside world. The Anglo world is verbal, so persuasive speaking and writing skills count. For students who do not live in language-rich environments, intercultural communication skills must be developed at school. Critical thinking requires the ability to make decisions, evaluate, and make judgments. The Hispanic cultural orientation of deference to authority or group frustrates teachers who want students to learn how to analyze information and develop their own opinions. As one Anglo teacher puts it, "Life is not a comfortable niche that you find and forever remain [in]. It is something that changes dynamically every day. And how you react to it depends on how well you prepare yourself to analyze—to look at it, to investigate it, to react to it." Some teachers want the school to take more responsibility for addressing all facets of children's development—social, cultural, emotional, intellectual, physical. Remoteness has not spared Norteño the travails that tear at the social fabric of other American communities. Resiliency and self-esteem need to be nurtured so students can better deal with home life problems—divorce, remarriage, abuse, poverty, alcoholism. As in other communities, people in Norteño disagree about whether the school or families should provide information about teen pregnancy prevention, support for teen moms, and AIDS. Some teachers think that students need more spirituality and moral education.

Academic subjects have displaced vocational training as the top priority in the Norteño School District, and the drop-out rate reflects the discouragement of those students who perform better with their hands. Part of the push for academics came from state legislative mandates in the 1980s, like Senate Bill 106,[3] and part from the stigma of manual labor. Some board of education members regret the abolition of auto mechanics, by which act they opened more time in the curriculum for reading and writing.

The industrial arts teacher disagrees with the school's emphasis on academics. On Mr. Martínez's workshop wall a poster fights the myth that vocational education graduates do not get good jobs:

> Only 20% of all jobs available in the year 2,000 will require four or more years of college. Approximately 60% of the remaining jobs will require the technical training found in secondary and post-secondary vocational training programs.

Mr. Martínez takes his students annually to visit Albuquerque's Technology and Vocational Institute to show them a vocational alternative. He requires students to research and write about topics related to industrial arts to prepare them for the continuing need for retraining: "These kids don't read. They should develop the habit of hobby reading and read

---

[3]The 1986 New Mexico State Legislature enacted major school reforms through Senate Bill 106. Section 1: F—"It is the purpose of this reform legislation ... to stress the importance of substantive academic subjects, provide for a greater emphasis on the primary grades, upgrade curriculum and graduation requirements, systematically evaluate instructional improvement and student progress, increase parental involvement in the public schools and recognize that teachers should be treated like other professionals."

a magazine cover to cover each week to keep them aware of change and ready for change."

Staff, students, and parents complain about the school's inadequacies. A missing "R" in the curriculum is research, because of insufficient library and laboratory facilities. Financial constraints keep the school's libraries locked evenings, weekends, and over the summer. Computer networking and acquisitions lag behind the times. Moreover, no honors courses are offered, and few enrichment activities scheduled for the summer. Geographical inaccessibility puts students at a serious disadvantage because it limits work opportunities. This limitation prevents students from integrating practical experiences and service learning programs with their studies.

There are gaps in Spanish instruction after the elementary bilingual program. No middle school Spanish courses are offered, and Spanish is taught only as a foreign language in high school, with more emphasis on grammar than on literature, culture, or conceptual knowledge. Graduation requirements include only one unit of Spanish. The limited levels of Spanish instruction mix students of different abilities; if teachers pace classes for the slower learners, the more advanced students may be bored. A few teachers think that Spanish should not be taught as a foreign language, because the textbooks present standard Spanish and depict Latin American or Iberian histories and lifestyles. These teachers suggest creating curricular materials that maintain Northern New Mexican Spanish and portray Hispano stories about place, history, and folkways.

Much of the focus of the bilingual debates has been on cultural issues, but there are also linguistic issues. A bilingual program initiated with federal Title VII and state funds is operational in grades K to 6, and each classroom is assigned a bilingual teaching assistant. A Spanish language maintenance curriculum guide exists but, ironically, is not used much. One reason for the lack of use is that teachers disagree about how to address the students' Language Assessment Scale scores. These scores indicate that nearly 70% of Norteño's students lack proficiency in English, and more are inadequate in Spanish. Many speak English using the Spanish linguistic structure. Some teachers worry that limited bilingualism, characterized by low proficiency in both languages, results in negative cognitive consequences due to poor reading and writing skills. They argue for developing strong literacy skills in one language first, but they disagree about which should be the first language.

The state department of education proposes integrating biliteracy throughout the K to 12 curriculum. Some teachers disagree, preferring that the elementary school create the developmental environment for biliteracy and biculturalism, while the secondary school emphasize content areas and English. Some elementary teachers believe that children must have a dominant language on which to build and transfer knowledge. These teachers suggest emphasizing critical thinking skills that will later transfer from one language into another rather than spending time trying to develop bilingual skills at such a young age. Other teachers think that enriching the language environment of children through a simultaneous bilingual approach will improve the students' overall literacy skills.

Supporters of the dual language immersion program push for structured learning of English and Spanish from the first day of elementary school. They believe that rooting the curriculum in the daily lives of students will build a foundation for cultural growth, advocacy, and dealing with change. The promise of their approach is that it teaches students cross-cultural communication and how to influence social change. It gives conflict, difference, and change legitimate places in the educational process; it encourages students to take a stance on issues and to be in charge of their own lives. Such a curriculum would include studying how culture determines human behavior and social inequity (Griego-Jones, 1996; Sleeter & Grant, 1988).

With this kaleidoscope of student needs, creating a suitable curriculum is a challenge. "Considerations of fit" arise from differences of opinion about whether to develop public or private individuality, or both (Peshkin, 1992).[4] Public individuality resides in the domain of the Anglo culture; private individuality in the domain of the Hispano culture. In Norteño schools, the two cultural orientations compete to be the "host culture"—the dominant cultural lens through which students view themselves.

Different endorsements of what is fit can undervalue aspects of both cultures and create a gap on the basis of what is not learned at school—the "null curriculum" (Eisner, 1979). Contention about the explicit, implicit, and null curricula continue in the Norteño School District, because the two cultural commitments have different premises about the well-being of the students. Curricular trade-offs and accommodations between the two cultural orientations are being overlooked, ignored, or resisted:

---

[4]Alan Peshkin (1992) used the concept of "fit" to consider what types of curricula suit different cultural orientations in "The Relationship Between Culture and Curriculum: A Many Fitting Thing."

The fact that one group's good fit is another group's misfit indicates the desirability of cost-benefit analyses that ask, What is lost in the course of gaining something else? Do the gains amply compensate the losses, and how can such estimations be made? Who is benefiting and who is losing? (Peshkin, 1992, p. 262)

Teachers are making scattered efforts to reach a consensus about the role the school could play in serving the social and cultural interests of the community. However, tension persists. Teachers who endorse the Anglo orientation want a rigorous curriculum that will prepare their students to cope with life in contexts larger than Norteño; they want young Norteños to be on par with Anglos in college and in the workforce. Teachers who endorse the Hispano orientation see cultural distinctness as an advantage, as well as a necessity for cultural revival, the viability of the villages, and the well-being of each individual. In their view, being different from the Anglo mainstream is worth the potential social, economic, and political costs.

Other educators prefer a bicultural orientation that teaches adolescents to function competently in both cultures and "to distinguish situations where traditional ethnic behaviors are appropriate from those where a mainstream system is more useful" (Rotheram-Borus, 1993, p. 89). Although being able to walk in two worlds seems ideal, critics argue that this approach oversimplifies "the tremendous internal conflict that can ensue when an individual tries to live according to two value systems that in some ways contradict each other" (Henze & Vanett, 1993, p. 124). It masks the complexity of choices faced. It assumes that only two worlds exist, that people pursue the best of both worlds, and that schools act as mediators between traditional and mainstream cultures.

Followers of each of these orientations advocate social change through schooling, but from different vantage points. Their differences illustrate the compromises schools make when they take on, implicitly or explicitly, the role of cultural mediator. How would a school demonstrate that it values the language and culture of both worlds? How much immersion is necessary for children to choose what is best from each world? Do we assume that the two cultures exhibit internal uniformity and that people would agree on what is the best of either culture or of both? Or that cultural identity, based on self-selected knowing and valuing, can be individually constructed in a space between the two worlds?

The interactions between teachers and students, sometimes referred to as the "hidden curriculum," take on greater importance if teachers view their classrooms as arenas to lobby for a particular cultural orientation (Hernández, 1989). The curricular approaches of teachers reflect their "sense of what is good in the curriculum that should be perpetuated, of what is missing and should be included, and of what is included but not in the right degree or right way and should be modified" (Peshkin, 1992, p. 250). Deciding who should teach what to Norteño students depends on which cultural orientation predominates and which assumptions exist.

TEACHER FIT

[T]eaching ideology [is] a connected set of systematically related beliefs and ideas about what are felt to be the essential features of teaching.... [T]he concept is broad and encompasses both cognitive and evaluative aspects, including general ideas and assumptions about the nature of knowledge, human nature, society, the role and functions of education, the tasks teachers have to perform, and the criteria to assess adequate performance of students.

—Trujillo (1996, p. 126)

The Norteño community pressures the school district to hire locals, believing that their teaching ideology includes a long-term commitment to the district, caring for the students in a familial way, being intercultural brokers, and filling a niche previously occupied by outsiders. The Norteño School District uses the grow-your-own approach to bolster the ranks of qualified local teachers. Teaching assistants, mostly Hispanos, are hired as part of the bilingual program and are the population targeted to become homegrown teachers. Investing in their own community members promises a high yield—the viability of Norteño cultural knowledge in the schools.

One shortcoming of this approach is evident: Homegrown teachers may lack exposure to the outside world and to ways of teaching that are different from how they were taught. However, in response to the criticism about the inbreeding of ideas, a student comments that locals connect with students by relating personal stories: "The teachers from here share their own experiences about growing up here, going to school, what happened when they left the community, and what they wish they had known when they were teenagers." Although good role models in the classroom, few locals appear to use culture and lived experience as the context for social change. Rather than teaching students how to address social inequity, most local teachers emphasize learning cultural heritage.

In cultural terms, locals add continuity; outsiders diversity. Some residents support bringing in outsiders who can expose the students to new ideas and perspectives. Outsiders tend to emphasize critical thinking, competition, and individualism. Outsiders prefer classroom discussion, but some occasionally make incorrect assumptions about what Norteño students know. Some outsiders encounter hostility because their personal values challenge local values and ways of doing things; others are noted for the new perspectives they bring to students and for modeling good English skills. A few outsiders show little sensitivity to local culture, history, and norms. Teachers who come with an agenda to change Norteño often get discouraged and leave.

The concept of fit applies when the school district tries to determine the suitability and effectiveness of teachers. When the superintendent hires faculty from outside the area, he wants them to visit the community first to get a feel for the students' home environments and to consider what it means to teach in an isolated community with an Hispano majority. To understand what a good fit means in Norteño, I asked teachers, administrators, and students to describe what a teacher from outside Norteño should accept about the community. The following composite paraphrases and quotes their advice to outsiders about teacher fit.

***

An Hispanic teacher recalls when she first arrived in Norteño: "The three questions I was asked the most were: Are you a Catholic? Are you married? Do you speak Spanish?" Fitting in with locals means being like them. So what happens if you answer "no" to any of these questions, or you are not Hispanic?

Before signing a contract with the district, realize that teaching in Norteño will be a cross-cultural experience. "Understand the culture, live within it, and don't try to Anglicize us." Nothing puts off locals more than patronizing newcomers who try to dictate what's best for Norteños. Avoid attempting changes that conflict with local values. Locals are not willing to give up what they stand for.

"Remember you're moving into the community as well as the school. People are open and share, but it's a religious and conservative community. If you isolate yourself, people might think you feel you're better than they are." Acting too differently can offend. Accept the way of dressing, the food, and the feelings of community members, whether negative or positive. Be open to ideas presented by the community, and participate in community celebrations: weddings, fiestas, graduation, confirmations, and baptisms. Be sensitive to the pressure community expectations place on local teachers, who have to be accountable to friends and relatives.

Newcomers need to understand the nature of interethnic contact in the area and why negative attitudes prevail in some corners. Being labeled "Anglo" can be uncomfortable for people who are not used to being defined by their ethnicity or who have never encountered anti-Anglo sentiments. Don't feel threatened by difference. Locate ethnic boundaries and abide by them, noting that with time, the boundaries often shift. Problems between Anglo teachers and non-Anglo students sometimes are considered racial. Be forewarned, "If an outsider hurts a student, you have the whole community, not just the parents and kid, to answer to." If you cannot accept the culture in the first year, leave.

To work in the Norteño School District, a teacher needs a working knowledge of Spanish and bilingual certification. Learn to speak the local vernacular, and recognize the limitations of *mocho*, the local manner of mixing Spanish and English. Don't criticize people for perceived backwardness or confuse Norteños with recent immigrants from Mexico. "If you show any prejudice, you won't last long."

Understand the upbringing and social environments of the students. Many of the students are from welfare families, so the school's goal is to motivate them to become self-sufficient. Find ways to work their experiences and feelings into the curriculum. In the classroom, students expect teachers to interact with them, not just assign readings and worksheets. "Set high expectations and teach like you really want to make a difference, but respect students even if they don't meet your standards. Show us you're here for the students, not the money."

***

"Don't try to Anglicize us." One hundred years after the first Protestant missionary arrived in Norteño, the community expects newcomers to not be culturally disruptive. Assimilationists, secular humanists, and school reformers receive cool welcomes. Monolingual teachers need not apply to teach Norteño children. To an outsider, Norteños might appear "as stagnant captives of tradition" rather than as "creators who have been fashioning their adaptations for three centuries or more, and who show the capacity to continue to change and create without ceasing to be Hispanos" (Kutsche, 1979a, p. 19). Teacher fit requires acceptance of who Norteños are and want to become.

Prospective teachers need to understand how to identify the nature of the relationship between a rural community and its school; they need to learn how to enhance that relationship. Who teaches what and how they teach will help shape the content, form, and boundaries of ethnic groups in Norteño. How the school district, faculty, and families choose to treat ethnicity will affect the ethnic identity of students—their awareness, acceptance, or rejection of native ethnic status or their compromise with it. Learning to become continues to be a complex process in which students rediscover and select from their cultural past and choose from multiple messages about the future.

6

A Fitting School: The Politics of Language and Identity

> The battlefields of multiculturalism are the borderlands between cultures, between social classes, between groups.
> —Anzaldúa (1992)

In 1961, anthropologist Florence Kluckhohn predicted that the Hispanic cultures in Northern New Mexico would disappear, given the pressures for assimilation: "There can be no turning back by these people, given the facts that they are firmly held within the borders of the United States and increasingly subjected to Anglo-American culture" (Manuel, 1965, p. 35). Kluckhohn could not have anticipated the cultural resistance of the *La Raza* movement that would crystallize in Northern New Mexico in the 1970s as strong opposition to the federal government's refusal to return or compensate for land acquired from communal Spanish land grants. The resurgence of ethnic pride and the state's mandate for multicultural education are altering, but not stopping, the course of Kluckhohn's prediction. In the community of Norteño, there are differing views of how the school should address multiculturalism. Each view depicts a different role for the school in mediating cultural change; each holds a different notion of what constitutes a fitting school for Norteño children.

Hispano autonomy over the Norteño School District has not spared Norteño from being a battlefield of multiculturalism where remaining and becoming are not reconciled. In this community where the resident majority is a minority in the outside world, no precedent exists to predict where individuals will fall on the assimilation continuum. The current debates in Norteño about bilingual education reflect past debates about casting schools in the implicit role of cultural mediator—that is, expecting schools to initiate, pace, and respond to cultural change in relation to movements, structures, and discourses beyond the school (Levinson & Holland, 1996).

In this final chapter, I explore how the politics of language and identity affect Norteño's struggle to agree on how to help their children position themselves for the future. Educational solutions depend on whether Norteños view language as a problem, language as a right, or language as a resource for such positioning (Ovando, 1999; Yzaguirre, 1998). Norteño reminds us that language has symbolic power, as well as its instructional and practical functions, in society (Griego-Jones, 1996).

LANGUAGE POLITICS:
LANGUAGE AS A PROBLEM, RIGHT, RESOURCE

Legislating Language

The language issue in New Mexico's schools has been in the political arena ever since the territorial days. School policy has vacillated in accordance with mandates for school instruction to be monolingual in English or bilingual in Spanish and English. By an act of Congress in 1910, the territory received permission to set up a government with a provision "for the establishment and maintenance of a system of public schools, which shall be open to all children ... and free from sectarian control, and that such schools shall always be conducted in English" (Moyers ,1941, p. 467). The mandate for English as the language of instruction reflected the political sentiment of the late 19th century, which equated proficiency in English with patriotic loyalty.

New Mexico struggled for statehood at a time when Theodore Roosevelt included language differences in his attacks on "hyphenated Americanism": "We have room for but one language in this country and that is the English language, for we intend to see that the crucible turns our people out as Americans, of American nationality, and not as dwellers in a polyglot boarding house" (Crawford, 1989/1991, p. 23).

But when statehood came to New Mexico in 1912, Hispano delegates at the constitutional convention in Santa Fe defended the heritage and civil rights of the Spanish-speaking people in New Mexico (Meier & Rivera, 1972). They succeeded in getting a constitutional provision to ensure that Spanish-speaking children would not be segregated in schools:

Children of Spanish descent in the state of New Mexico shall never be denied the right and privilege of admission and attendance in the public schools or other public education institutions of the State, and they shall never be classed in separate schools, but shall forever enjoy perfect equality with other children in all public schools and educational institutions of the State (Constitution of the State of New Mexico, 1912, art. 12, sec. 10).

Ahead of the times, New Mexico mandated bilingual teacher training, but with inconsistent enforcement.

Soon after New Mexico achieved statehood, conscription for World War I took Hispano youth away from their village homes. Most frequently, teachers and graduates of mission schools were drafted, but less-educated Hispanos were tapped as well. It was a measure of the isolation of the Norteños that conscription provided some with their first contact with the United States government and the Pledge of Allegiance; some did not know enough English to follow military drills.

Wartime patriotism increased support for promoting English as the official language of the United States. The campaign for "Americanism" fueled the Protestant missionaries in New Mexico, who proclaimed,

[T]he tongue of the state is Spanish, and we do not want one flag, one country, and two languages, but "one flag, one country, and one language." Reinforced in this way, Americanization came to play an increasing, though not a new role in missionary endeavors, dampening whatever fires of pluralism may have glowed before the war. (Deutsch, 1987, p. 112)

In spite of the Americanization movement the war effort inspired, New Mexican legislators passed a law in 1915 that attempted to circumvent the English-only statehood provision and to enforce the bilingual education statute in schools like those in the northern villages. The new law stipulated that Spanish be taught as a separate subject in public schools if a majority vote of a district's board of education indicated desire for such instruction. Textbooks were to be in the English language, "provided that Spanish may be used in explaining the meaning of English words to Spanish-speaking pupils who do not understand English" (Moyers, 1941, p. 497). Another section of the new law allocated funds to train 50 native Spanish-speaking teachers at the Spanish-American school, established in the northern village of El Rito in 1909. This Normal School provided many inhabitants of Rio Arriba and Taos Counties their first opportunity to attend school beyond the fourth grade (Deutsch, 1987; Wagner, 1920).

Politicians continued to debate the linguistic welfare of Spanish-speaking children. Their concerns have a contemporary ring. In 1917, they made it unlawful to certify teachers who refused to comply with a board of education's mandate "to teach reading in Spanish and English by the bilingual methods to all pupils in the first, second, and third grades" (Moyers, 1941, p. 497). A more stringent law, passed in 1919, required teachers in Hispanic schools to be proficient in reading, writing, and speaking both English and Spanish. In 1923, the English-only clause of 1891 was finally repealed.

Forgotten Students: Educational Inequality

Having bilingual instruction laws on the books did not guarantee education of equal quality for Spanish-speaking students. George Sanchez (1906–1972), a psychology professor and prominent Hispano researcher from the University of New Mexico, worked for 40 years to remedy the deficiencies in the education of Spanish-speaking children. Sanchez claimed that Hispanos were cast aside as the by-product of imperialism. Throughout Sanchez's professional career, he advocated cultural dualism, criticizing the government for not meeting the special needs of Spanish-speaking citizens (Chavarria, 1977).

In 1940, Sanchez published *Forgotten People: A Study of New Mexicans*. Comparing education in New Mexico with education in other states in terms of economic support and pupil achievement, Sanchez found New Mexico third from the bottom. Using 1938 school statistics, Sanchez found that Spanish-speaking children made up half the state school population but only one fifth of the 12th-grade enrollment. The figures indicated that more than half of the Spanish-speaking children enrolled in Taos County schools were in the first three grades (Sanchez, 1940/1967, pp. 30–31). At that time, Norteño's 9 teachers taught 300 children in the elementary grades and 70 in the high school.

Why did so few Spanish-speaking students graduate from high school in the counties with the largest proportions of Spanish-speaking people? Sanchez concluded that Spanish-speaking children were systematically forced out of schools by lack of state support. Compared with other schools in the state, the schools serving Spanish-speaking regions of Northern New Mexico had shorter school terms, inferior school buildings and materials of instruction, less well prepared teachers, and lower teacher salaries (Sanchez, 1940/1967, p. 31). Having begun teaching with only a high school diploma, Sanchez knew firsthand about under-qualified teachers. He had felt unprepared to deal with the eight grades of Spanish-speaking children he taught in a one-room rural school. Other teachers had started with fewer qualifications. As of the 1940s, only 46% of the teachers in the Hispanic counties had college degrees, compared to 82% of the teachers in the Anglo counties (Fincher, 1974, p. 68). Many of the teachers without college degrees were graduates of the El Rito Spanish-American Normal School, which unlike other teacher training institutions, did not offer collegiate courses (Moyers, 1941). An elder in Norteño recalls a teacher with poor credentials:

> When I was a child, I went to school in the village. The teacher himself had not finished the eighth grade, but he had quite a bit of good connections with the local board. So year after year, just before school ended, he made it a point to ask for reinstatement for the next year. So he taught for a good number of years. I remember, too, that the wife of the teacher would take over while the teacher in the spring would do his planting. She had no certification whatsoever. She knew very little English (personal communication, October 29, 1992).

Sanchez's battle for equal education brought him notoriety in the 1930s when he began attacking the notion that Spanish-speaking children are inherently intellectually inferior to English-speaking children, as indicated by differences in IQ scores. Sanchez questioned whether the tests, drawn from the notion of an average child, measured what they purported to measure. He argued that schools are responsible for creating experiences for bilingual children that make the knowledge sampled by the IQ test as common to them as to the Anglo children from whose test scores the norms are derived. Simply translating the tests from English to Spanish is not enough (Lopez & Samora, 1977; Murillo, 1977).

Sanchez conceived of bilingual/bicultural education as a program linking school to familiar situations in the lives of students—their customs, traditions, history, and home language. He believed that curricular irrelevancy contributed to the high rate of school failure among Spanish-speaking children. A study of El Cerrito, a Spanish-American village, identified the problem of curricular irrelevancy:

> Such subject matter as geography, history, and health, is taught in terms that are foreign to the [Spanish Americans]. During the school year of 1939–40, the pupils of El Cerrito worked on posters and other projects based on such subjects as transportation in Boston and the importance of navigation in the growth of Chicago. Under such a curriculum as this, it is

small wonder that pupil interest is at a minimum and that progress is slow. (Leonard & Loomis, 1941, cited in Carter, 1970, p. 108)

Sanchez and other educators recommended a bicultural curriculum that built on the students' own cultural background and language. However, not all Hispanics agreed with Sanchez's bilingual/bicultural stance. During the 1930s, New Mexico's Senator Chavez pushed to have Spanish-speaking children taught exclusively in English. He worried that bilingual education would marginalize the Hispanic children, limiting their potential to compete with Anglo Americans. Chavez believed that the omission of English instruction in Northern New Mexican schools was intended to deprive students of a "weapon to fight back with" (Acuña, 1988; Fincher, 1974; González 1967).

The issue being debated then was the same as the one today: whether the Spanish language is a problem or a resource. As rural areas continued to decline economically and more people moved into the cities, a greater emphasis was placed on staying in school and learning English, frequently at the expense of Spanish: "People were being made moderately literate in a language they seldom used while being left quite illiterate in the language they commonly spoke" (Kluckhohn & Strodtbeck, 1961, p. 247).[1] This problem was discussed at the 1943 Conference on the Problems of Education Among Spanish-speaking Populations of Our Southwest, held at the University of New Mexico:

> The attractiveness of the Anglo American cultural pattern, especially in its material aspects, for an isolated people is so great that it constantly tends to assimilate them, willingly or unwillingly. The new generations clearly show the confusion brought about by the two forces acting upon them, one centripetal which prompts them for self preservation to take refuge in their own culture in the face of the unkindness of the dominant culture, and another centrifugal which prompts them to imitate the Anglo Americans. (Fincher, 1974, p. 71)

Advocacy for Language-Minority Students

The political mood of the 1960s brought into question the assumptions of the melting pot-conformist ethic in American culture, some argued "that *equal treatment* for children of limited English proficiency—in

---

[1]Kluckhohn and Strodtbeck made this statement in reference to their observations from fieldwork in Atrisco, New Mexico (1936–1957).

other words, 'submersion' in mainstream classrooms—meant *unequal opportunities* to succeed" (Crawford, 1989/1991, p. 34).[2] Such sentiments led to the landmark Bilingual Education Act of 1968. With this act, the U.S. Congress adopted a compensatory outlook toward poor Americans whose mother tongue was not English. President Lyndon B. Johnson signed this historic bill (S. 428) into law with these words:

> Thousands of children of Latin descent, young Indians, and others will get a better start—a better chance—in school.... What this law means, is that we are now giving every child in America a better chance to touch his outermost limits—to reach the farthest edge of his talents and his dreams. We have begun a campaign to unlock the full potential of every boy and girl—regardless of his race or his region or his father's income. (Andersson, 1973, p. 6)

This legislation paved the way for the New Mexico Bilingual Multicultural Act of 1973, drafted by the state board of education. At the time, New Mexico had a larger proportion of minority children in its public schools than any state in the nation, and only 1% of Norteño's students were Anglo.[3] George Sanchez's belief in cultural dualism was reflected in the new Act's cultural pluralism policy: "Every individual has a right to retain and expand his identity, his culture, and his language, and to participate in various cultural forms and values" (von Maltitz, 1975, p. 140). Senator Chavez's concerns about Spanish-speakers losing a competitive edge were also reflected in the policy's stipulation that bilingual–multicultural programs in public schools "must include specific objectives for developing complete functionality in English for all students so that they will be proficient in the national language" (von Maltitz, 1975, p. 140).

To implement the Bilingual Multicultural Act, the state hired a director from Puerto Rico, who brought to New Mexico the Miami Linguistics program designed to meet the second-language needs of Cubans who fled to Miami after the 1959 revolution in their homeland (Andersson, 1973).[4] The Miami program placed Cuban children in bilingual classrooms with

---

[2]Mary McGroarty (1992) also discussed the effect that the civil rights movement had on bilingual education in "The Societal Context of Bilingual Education."

[3]According to the *New Mexico School District Profile* (State Department of Education, 1971), 46.2% of all children in the state were minority children, of whom 37.0% were Spanish surname, 7.1% were Indian, and 2.1% were Negro. Children in Norteño School District were 97% Spanish surname, 2% Indian, and 1% Anglo.

[4]The contemporary period of bilingual schooling in the United States was inaugurated in the Coral Way Elementary School, Dade County, Miami, Florida, where a school population equally divided between English-speakers and Spanish-speaking Cubans were given a choice between the traditional all-English curriculum and bilingual programs in grades 1, 2, and 3.

English-speaking children, so that each could learn the other's language and work academically in both languages: "[T]he goal was to create functional bilinguals, who would maintain both languages through their school years.... The program was oriented toward enrichment of the child's linguistic and cultural experiences; it was not compensatory" (Hakuta, 1986, pp. 193–194). According to the superintendent who served in Norteño during the implementation of this program, the two-way bilingual approach proved to be a curricular mismatch for Norteño, which lacked what the Cubans had—large numbers of English-speaking students, well-educated parents, and well-trained bilingual teachers who spoke the same dialect of Spanish as the children.

In the 1970s, litigation and growing Hispanic political clout provided strong support for bilingual programs that would maintain the native language and promote fluency in two languages rather than just one. The politics of identity became apparent in schools:

> Bilingual education [was] arousing passions about the issues of political power and social status that are far removed from the classroom.... For some, bilingual education was strictly a remedial effort, designed to overcome children's "language deficiency" and to assimilate them quickly into the mainstream. For others, it was an enrichment program, intended to develop students' linguistic resources and to preserve their cultural heritage. (Crawford, 1989/1991, p. 13)

Contested Rights About Language

Adversaries of this resurgence in ethnic pride believed that bilingual education threatened the common language of the United States, English. Opponents of bilingual education contended that language minorities were un-American and a menace to our national culture. They claimed that cultural pluralism was a private matter of personal choice, not a responsibility of the schools and federal government. They criticized the legal link minorities established between bilingual education and affirmative action—the concept that affirmation of native language and culture in the school promotes self-esteem and encourages achievement. They attacked language maintenance programs for endorsing separatism (Epstein, 1977).

U.S. English, organized in 1983 by Hawaii's Senator S. I. Hayakawa and Michigan opthalmologist John Tanton for the purpose of promoting English as the official language, campaigned in New Mexico with the stated goals of avoiding bi-illiteracy and separatism. While Arizona and Colorado approved bills giving English official status, the New Mexico legislature defeated similar legislation in 1987. Many issues intersect in the controversy over English as the official language: immigration, the rights of minorities, recognition of ethnicity as a special status in public education, the pedagogical value of bilingual education, the place of cultural diversity in school curricula, and tolerance in American society (Hakuta, 1986; King, 1997).

Critics of the English-only movement dispute language restrictionism and the notion that being an American means speaking English (Rodriguez, 1991). The countervailing English-Plus coalition maintains that the national interest would be better served by encouraging mastery of English *plus* other languages. In 1988 the U.S. Congress created a $55 million program to promote the teaching of foreign languages and, paradoxically, a nearly $90 million program for transitional bilingual education designed to replace other languages with English (Crawford, 1989/1991; Hernández, 1989). The social and political forces that frame the debates about bilingual education in Norteño reflect the federal confusion of simultaneously promoting pluralism and monoculturalism.

AFFIRMING ETHNICITY

Who stands to gain? To understand the politics of identity in Northern New Mexico, I again turn to local authors and the literature on ethnicity to consider what it means for cultural boundaries to shift from generation to generation. The issue of affirming ethnicity through linguistic difference divides the Norteño community. In a newspaper article titled "Hispanics Must Learn English or Fall Further Behind," Philip Vargas, a Northern New Mexican whose first language was Spanish, recalled growing up in his isolated mountain community and feeling the indignity of being at the mercy of those who spoke English. In the article, he addressed Spanish-speaking readers with a difficult question:

> The question the [bilingual] issue poses for Hispanic-Americans is this: Do we truly wish to make American society *our* society, or do we prefer to remain the shadow people? Do we really intend to participate fully and make our individual contributions to America's experiment in self-realization and self-government? Or will we remain in the back of the auditoriums, quiet and passive, because of misplaced fear that moving to center stage will cost us our language and culture?... Preserving our language and culture is a good thing, to be sure, but if it keeps our children from benefiting

from the opportunities available in this rich society, then these cultural factors—these barriers within ourselves—may have to be modified. (Vargas, 1991, p. 9A)

Vargas' words are a caution to cultural preservationists to consider whether their language and culture enhance or inhibit access to the public arena.

Other Hispanos assert that greater political power comes from maintaining ethnic boundaries. Faced with today's diversity in Northern New Mexico, their call to defend the *Manito* nation—the brotherhood of Hispanos—is urgent.[5] Activist Juan Estevan Arellano has been throwing up dust for over 20 years against the mad dash of modern living and the encroachment of Anglo economic development ventures that have led some Norteños to forsake time-honored traditions involving agriculture, socializing, local history, extended families, and folklore. His publication, *arellano*, is committed to keeping the past alive in the present, to organizing resistance against change, to creating a space for the expression of Hispano cultural and linguistic difference, and to preserving subsistence farming culture. Writing in the Spanish of *paisanos norteños* (northern village natives), he fights for *querencia*—love of home, an anchor to the ground (Abel, 1997).[6]

Other authors also champion linguistic difference. Nasario García of New Mexico Highlands University battled with editors to publish Río Puerco Valley *cuentos* as told in the local Spanish.[7] Later he received high praise from reviewers for the authenticity of language in *Abuelitos: Stories of the Rio Puerco Valley*, published in 1992. In *Dancing to Pay the Light Bill*, Jim Sagel, an Anglo married to an Hispana, defends the local

---

[5] In *Los Manitos* (1957), Munro Edmonson explained that Old Mexicans used to refer to New Mexicans as *manito*, short for *hermanito*—little brother. I was told by Dr. Cecilio Orozco at the 1993 New Mexico State Bilingual Conference that people used to greet each other using *Mano* or *Mana* before their names to signify the strong sentiment of brotherand sisterhood in the community.

[6] On the inside cover of *Querencia*, Stephen Bodio (1990) quoted William F. Buckley's definition of *querencia* : "The word doesn't translate. It is used in Spanish to designate that mysterious little area in the bullring that catches the fancy of the fighting bull when he charges in. He imagines it his sanctuary: when parked there, he supposes he cannot be hurt.... So it is, borrowing the term, that one can speak of one's '*querencia*' to mean that little, unspecified area in life's arena where one feels safe, serene."

[7] In 1911, Aurelio Espinosa raised the concern about Northern New Mexican Spanish being deprived of the literary culture that enriches a language in "The Spanish Language in New Mexico and Southern Colorado." The article described distinguishing characteristics of the colloquial Spanish, the influences of other languages, and morphological changes.

Spanglish from those who claim that mixing languages means double illiteracy. He describes Spanglish as a social construct, grounded in social interaction:

The bilingual speaker is like a *pintor* [painter] with two sets of *colores* [colors].... It's 'Spanglish' that allows the young Hispanic to bridge the two *mundos* [worlds] of his daily existence, keeping him afloat in contemporary society and, yet, in touch with his *raíces* [roots].... It is, after all, the *jóvenes* [youth] who find themselves on the front lines of cultural upheaval.... The linguistic doomsayers may weep in their *diccionarios* [dictionaries] all they want: they cannot stop the spread of 'Spanglish.' For all language is quicksilver, a constantly evolving mirror of reality. As long as the southwestern *espejo* [mirror] reflects two cultural systems in daily collision and collusion, people will speak bilingually.[8] (Sagel, 1992, pp. 6–8)

Norteño is a cultural borderland where a minority culture evolves internally while competing externally with the nation's mass culture for opportunities and survival. Some argue that preservation lies in tourism, the daily collusion between the Anglo and Hispano cultures. Presenting aspects of their lifestyle in museum-like exhibits allows Hispanos to stay in their communities. On the other hand, Sylvia Rodriguez, a *Taoseña* [native of Taos] and an anthropologist at the University of New Mexico, has cited research that shows how dependency on tourism has profoundly affected the self-image of Hispanos and Pueblo Indians. She warns against the negative process of "reconstructed ethnicity"—molding one's definition of self to fit another's perception of oneself. Essentially, a brokering of cultural characteristics goes on between the minority and majority cultures. If a cultural trait sells or entertains, it defines and represents the minority group's ethnic identification. Thus, the Anglo attraction reinforces ethnic boundaries by confining the dynamic nature of Hispano culture and the potential for self-definition by Hispanos (Rodriguez, 1987).

For the more radical, slowing the tide of cultural change means putting up barriers. In "Surviving in the 21st Century: My Dreams, Hopes, Wishes for the Survival of the Río Arriba," María Mondragón-Valdez (1992) raised this question: "How will the quality of life be altered if we are marketed as tourist attractions?" She then argued for real boundaries to be established around Northern New Mexican villages that de-

---

[8]The English translation is not in the original text.

clare the land "off limits to tourists, mining companies, recreational developers, dude ranches, 'People for the West' types, golf courses, and subdivisions" (Mondragón-Valdez, 1992, pp. 18–19). She suggested forming a regional watch group to guard against being seduced into selling land for short-term gains and to monitor the environmental impact of development activities. A more extreme strategy for cultural survival is the youth camp in Tierra Amarilla, where a few young Hispanics and Blacks learn about "an upcoming revolution against ... a common oppressor—the affluent White ruling class that has taken their land and diluted their culture" (Stieber, 1992, p. A19).

COMPETING LOCAL AND NATIONAL INTERESTS

Norteño stands at the junction: Whose interests should a school represent? The debate about local or national interests, decentralized or standardized education, goes back to when the nation urbanized at the end of the 19th century. The major arguments from that time sound much like the arguments today for why rural schools should conform to a uniform system of education: "[A] standard education must be offered to all children if they [are] all to be equally able to take advantage of the economic opportunities offered by the urban centers" (Dunne, 1983, p. 253). Gradually, state and federal regulations about teacher certification, curriculum content, graduation requirements, building standards, and funding have eroded the ability of local school boards to act in the local interest. Local school boards spend most of their time trying to figure out how to comply with such regulations.

Barriers to Local Control

Can Norteño move toward more local control in spite of recent initiatives to develop national standards? Ideally, national standards would balance national direction with local discretion and foster educational equity by providing additional resources to schools in poor areas. But the move toward national standards focuses on the development of instructional materials, appropriate means of assessment, and accountability rather than on local flexibility (Smith, O'Day, & Cohen, 1990).[9] To some

---

[9]Marshall S. Smith, Jennifer O'Day, and David K. Cohen (1990) considered whether a national curriculum is feasible and what it might look like in an article titled "National Curriculum American Style."

Norteños, the national standards movement resembles the English-only movement, which places national interests above local ones.

Outcome-based education offers schools some flexibility to consider the cultural context of the community, but opinions about local control are often overshadowed by the spending guidelines of federal and state funding agencies. Such funding sources usually offer only short-term interventions prescribed by educational experts who define equal educational opportunity without reference to local control. In essence, funding specifications become the tail that wags the curriculum in school districts. For example, the bilingual program in Norteño alone constitutes 10% of the district's operational costs, and the district's reliance on 3-year bilingual grants impedes the development of a long-term bilingual program designed to meet the community's needs. Compliance mechanisms associated with federal educational funds inadvertently displace local choice and initiative. No lasting restructuring or reform occurs, and outside funding perpetuates dependency.

An article in *The Christian Science Monitor* disclosed the funding sources for New Mexico public schools: local—11.2%, state—76.1%, federal—12.7% (Walters, 1994). New Mexico is second to last nationally for local funding of schools, and Norteño's funding formula offers even less local control—1% of the budget comes from residential and nonresidential taxes, 86% from the state, and 13% from federal sources. Although only approximately $2,000 of the Norteño's School District's revenue is generated from residential taxes, the board of education finds bond issues a hard sell. In 1987 and 1992, Norteño residents voted down a a two-mill levy that would have taxed property $2 per thousand of the assessed value. Although a bond issued for $210,000 passed in 1982, voters rejected a $725,000 school bond issue a decade later. The community's perception of school control explains the negative vote: "Schools are state facilities, so let the state finance them." But legislators interpret the community's rejection of the bond differently: "If the community does not want to help itself, why should the state help the community?" Bond and tax levy support finally won voter approval in the mid-1990s.

The inability to generate local funds prevents the school district from weaning itself from the dictates of other sources of funding. In a sparsely populated state with an average per capita income of $11,250, income and sales taxes hold little hope for generating enough revenue for schools. The skyrocketing property taxes in Santa Fe and Taos have led to legislative efforts, like California's Proposition 13, to cap property tax rates at the 1990 assessments, thereby limiting the availability of local funding even more.[10]

A Community School Concept

Should the Norteño School District develop a curriculum that links the school with community revitalization? In Northern New Mexico, the school as the focal point of community development is not a novel idea. Hispanic New Deal programs like the Taos County Project (1940–1943) involved rural people in finding solutions to their own problems through cooperative efforts between community and school. Educators served as community liaisons for reporting needs, gathering information, and suggesting how to develop regional economic independence after the Great Depression. The project concentrated its efforts on creating a better life in the villages; educational debates centered on whether the curriculum should be tied to the farm or the nation.[11]

One of these New Deal programs, the Nambé Community School (1937–1942), was directed by University of New Mexico Professor Lloyd Tireman. Tireman attempted to change the school's role from "culture imposer" to "culture stimulator" by presenting the school as the center of community regeneration:

- We shall try to find out what is most needed in the lives of the people of this community and minister to that before all else.
- We shall constantly try to discover and utilize the resources of the community. The fields, arroyos, the homes, and the shops shall be a part of our laboratories, and [the community's] workers [shall be] among our teachers.

---

[10]Given that today approximately 60% of the nation's public school districts are rural, with populations averaging less than 2,500, alternative funding formulas make sense. These facts are listed in Section 2 of the Rural Schools of America Act (S. 1472), submitted by Senator Paul Simon, September 20, 1993.

[11]Information about Norteño's school enrollment and conditions was reported at Taos County Project meetings on June 13, 1941, and January 9, 1942. Copies of the minutes are in the Florence Ellis Collection, Center for Southwest Research, General Library, University of New Mexico. See J. T. Reid's *It Happened in Taos* (1946) for more information on the Taos County Project. These programs helped improve the educational work of agencies and organizations operating in the county: health education and services, agriculture and home economics courses, adult education, playgrounds, school hot lunch programs, libraries, educational movies, and a bookmobile that still comes to the communities.

• The starting point in every part of the curriculum will be Nambé.[12]
(Bachelor, 1990, p. 72)

Home visits identified community concerns: poor health conditions,
legal disputes over land ownership, soil conservation and land manage-
ment, coordinating government agency services, consumer education,
and reviving native craftsmanship to generate income. After only 5
years, the community voted to close the experimental Nambé Community School and return the elementary school to Santa Fe School District
jurisdiction. Opponents of the school claimed that channeling relief
funds into colonial crafts training kept the villagers isolated and fostered
a view of Hispano culture as static. Parents' apprehension about change
and their children's futures fueled the controversy: One village faction
criticized the school for not encouraging youngsters to stay at home; the
other faction faulted the school for not preparing students to join the national job market so they could enjoy more opportunities than their parents did. The school's closing ended Tireman's efforts to improve the
education of rural, Spanish-speaking New Mexicans (Bachelor, 1990).

So 50 years later the cycle of debate returns to the merits and draw-
backs of teaching Hispano culture in school. In the interplay between educational quality and educational control, rural children benefit from
curriculum choices made on behalf of local values: "The relationships
and loyalties formed in the school are expected to yield dividends in the
form of a new generation of local citizens who will support the values
that keep the community alive" (Dunne, 1983, p. 254). But there are reasons to make curricular decisions according to a national culture: Rural
children need to be exposed to nonlocal cultural norms, political ideology,
and economic expectations.

Preserving the Spanish language and culture remains a primary concern, and current debates in Norteño about bilingual education and assimilation continue to echo the earlier divergent opinions of George

---

[12]Dr. Tireman modeled the Nambé Community School after the San José Job Training
and Experimental School (1930–1935). The latter was a Carnegie Foundation rural education project with the goals of adapting a 640-pupil New Mexican school to serve as a community resource and developing the best instructional methods and materials for
non-English-speaking children. Dr. Tireman questioned the relevancy of the traditional
school curriculum: "Do our Spanish-speaking people need fractions, decimals, grammar?... Or do they need teachers who will show them how to plant proper vegetables, how
to achieve more economic freedom, how to feed their children properly, how to improve
community relations?" (Bachelor, 1990, p. 48). Georgia L. Lusk mentioned the work of the
laboratory school in her *Report of the State Superintendent of Public Instruction: For the
Eleventh Biennium Period Beginning July 1, 1930 and Ending June 30, 1932* (pp. 43–45).

Sanchez and Senator Chavez. Some Chicano activists lobby for colloquial Spanish to be taught in Norteño's schools; some bilingual supporters view standard Spanish as their common bond with other Hispanics; others support teaching both standard and colloquial Spanish. Fifty years after the University of New Mexico's Conference on the Problem of Education Among Spanish-Speaking Populations, the counter forces of cultural imitation and cultural self-preservation continue to clash in Norteño.

ETHNIC BOUNDARY MAINTENANCE

I arrived in Norteño on the day of the annual fiesta—a Catholic celebration corresponding with the neighboring pueblo's patron saint day. This tradition dates back to when the pueblo's mission church existed to convert the Indians, long before Norteño villagers constructed their own Catholic Church.[13] A parade of teenage fiesta royalty, remodeled cars, horsemen, *mariachis* [musicians], and floats passed through the village. Then the one road through town filled with bumper-to-bumper traffic and a bonanza of friends and relatives who had returned home for this annual ritual. They arrived from as far away as Wyoming and California. Their tenacious homeland bond—to people, place, and identity with place—is part of this story about remaining and becoming.

Even though today fewer people live off the land, land ownership has become a symbol of Hispano cultural survival. In her essay "Land, Water, and Ethnic Identity," Sylvia Rodriguez (1987) described the emergence of protest against displacement that began in the 1970s with land grant disputes and continues today.[14] Rodriguez's essay chronicled the Valdez condominium dispute, which went on from 1981 to 1982, just north of Taos. Roadside posters captured the anti-Anglo sentiment:

---

[13]Few villagers attended the pueblo's religious ceremonies that day. Sylvia Rodriguez (1996) described the tension that exists between the pueblo and Norteño about the Hispano community's carnival, dancing, and drinking during the Indians' religious celebration. A year after my fieldwork, a new priest finally pushed through an alcohol ban during the fiesta.

[14]Although the Treaty of Guadalupe Hidalgo guaranteed the property rights of Mexicans who chose to stay in Northern New Mexico, their practice of group land ownership did not coincide with the Anglo-American concept of individual land ownership. In the 1891 Forest Reserve Act, the federal government declared that the vast majority of land owned under common land grants would become public property and be set aside as national forests and parks. The Santa Fe National Forest was established in 1892; the Carson and Cibola National Forests in 1904. Although Hispanos retained village land and irrigated plots, they lost the use of their traditional grazing lands. The ensuing struggle over land between Anglo settlers and Spanish villagers fueled other power struggles and animosity between the two rival groups (Forrest, 1989; Friedman, 1978; Stoddard, 1973).

Commandments Against Condos

- Thou shall not build condos
- Thou shall not pollute our water
- Thou shall not disrespect our way of life
- Thou shall not pollute our land
- Thou shall not covet our land and water
- Thou shall not steal what belongs to our children
- Thou shall not kill our valley (Rodriguez, 1987, p. 325)

In her essay, Rodriguez focused on the increasing alignment of Norteño ethnic identity with the land and their strategies for maintaining ethnic boundaries:

[T]his ongoing process of expropriation and its recent acceleration have, in concert with various local, regional, and macrosocial factors, intensified rural Hispano resistance to further usurpation and displacement, and stimulated the crystallization of land as a symbol of Hispano cultural survival and social self-determination. (Rodriguez, 1987, p. 314)

Land grant litigations to halt Anglo encroachment and protests against realtors hanging out their shingles in the villages indicate Hispanos' feelings of exploitation: "Land is priceless. God isn't making any more. *Keep it!*"; "Land can be the biggest riches. You can give it to your children. Don't sell it, pass it on." In Norteño, protesters against a recent county zoning proposal feared that the proposed zoning would make the area more attractive to outsiders. They published a list of slogans: "Zoning is for the rich, not for the poor"; "Don't give your rights of your land to greedy people who seek control and power. You are doing great just as you are."

As a symbol, land represents a sense of being that is associated with a sense of place: the need "to feel like a placed person and not a displaced person" (Stegner, 1992, p. 12).[15] Hispanos reap cultural nourishment from the centuries-old process of cumulative association—staying long enough to put down roots and develop associations with a place: "No place is a place until things that have happened in it are remembered in history, ballads, yarns, legends, or monuments" (Stegner, 1992, p. 202). Knowing who you are comes from knowing where you are:

---

[15]In his collection of essays titled *When the Bluebird Sings to the Lemonade Springs: Living and Writing in the West,* Wallace Stegner (1992) embellished Wendell Berry's notion of the importance of place and being a "placed" person. Stegner described the importance of landscape in shaping the contours of people's lives.

... [A] kind of knowing that involves the senses, the memory, the history of a family ... [T]he knowledge of place that comes from working in it in all weathers, making a living from it, suffering from its catastrophes, loving its mornings or evenings or hot noons, valuing it for the profound investment of labor and feeling that you, your parents and grandparents, your all-but-unknown ancestors have put into it. (Stegner, 1992, p. 205)

Between 1980 and 1990, the Anglo population in Norteño's county increased from approximately 4,650 to 6,400 (38%), and the average value of housing increased 89% (Bureau of Business and Economic Research, 1992). When Anglos look to retire in the area, it drives up the real estate prices and forces the locals out. Not selling the land to outsiders is one Hispano strategy of resisting this trend. Cultural revival and retrenchment are forms of resistance against the prevailing Anglo commitment to change—the modern promise of success, with its imperatives of mobility, independence, adaptability, and capacity for continued growth.

Norteño residents have chosen to live here because of their belief in family, land, tradition, and culture. They take pride in their more humble existence that is tied to the seasons and the land. They see themselves as being able to tough it out in the winter and to live with some hardships. One senses their attachment to the land in the preparations made for winter—drying the *chicos* and *carne seca* [jerky], cutting wood, canning, and harvesting their *habas* [horsebeans]. Nevertheless, this strong attachment to the land is weakening.

When interviewed for a newspaper article about traditions jeopardized by the changing face of Northern New Mexico, activist Juan Estevan Arellano commented on those who turn away from agriculture and the communal lifestyle:

> People are not really connecting with the land as their parents did. People think if you work the land, you must not be able to work anywhere else. [They think] only the poor or the uneducated, those are the only people who work the land. (Parker, 1993, p. A1)

Arellano also lamented that the declining economic interdependence in Norteño reduces the common social interactions of rural life.[16] Without the land, people are not learning *cómo andar con la gente*—how one walks with the people.

---

[16]Rogelio Diaz-Guerrero (1987) discussed how the economic characteristics of a culture affect and are shaped by the historically established coping style of the culture in "Historical Sociocultural Premises and Ethnic Socialization."

Much of the research done in the 1970s about Northern New Mexico villages focused on the dilemma of out-migration as a response to economic pressures and opportunities.[17] Two decades later, an in-migration has brought back some native sons and daughters. Some are educated Norteños who returned to work as professionals in the school or neighboring communities or as entrepreneurs; others have returned because of retirement, the low cost of living, inherited land, or the chance to raise their children within the culture. Norteño is not just a "remnant society" composed of an aging population, as is the case in some Hispano communities (Nostrand, 1992; Weber, 1979). It has local employers, small businesses, and a large number of commuters who prefer to drive to work rather than move outside Norteño. The in- and out-migration of people helps Norteño retain its identity and reestablishes viable economic patterns in the community.

Economic and social changes alter the choices that direct Norteños' lives and the ethnic boundaries that shape their lives. Ethnic identity is a function of boundary maintenance: "Ethnicity is a matter of a double boundary, a boundary from within, maintained by the socialization process, and a boundary from without, established by the process of intergroup relations" (Barth, 1969, cited in Isajiw, 1974, p. 122).[18] This double boundary of ethnicity is shifting how Hispanos identify with others in Northern New Mexico. A lifestyle contained within the isolation of geographic boundaries served Norteños for over 250 years. Now the boundary from within is identified more by cultural traits—such as language, land, faith, and food—than by livelihood. The boundary from without depends on the nature of interactions with Anglos and the opportunities afforded and constraints imposed by the majority society.

Some 30 years ago, social scientists predicted that the last part of the 20th century would be characterized by a resurgence of ethnicity and race; few took them seriously. As the nation closes in on their homeland's borders, Hispanos are becoming more fragmented. Some choose to cross the cultural border; to them, ethnicity is a resource to turn to when they need strength to become. Some struggle to remain different and to belong on both sides of the border; for them, ethnicity is an eddy in the mainstream, majority culture. Others take a separatist stance on their own side of the

---

[17]See the collection of essays in *The Survival of Spanish American Villages*, edited by Paul Kutsche (1979b).

[18]Frederik Barth (1969) asserted that the focus of research on cultural differences should shift from looking at ethnic groups separately to analyzing the ethnic boundaries formed through intergroup attitudes and interactions.

border; ethnicity is a fortress that protects them and gives them the strength to remain through opposition to the dominant culture (Davidson et al., 1993). Depending on which ethnic metaphor a Norteño chooses, the boundary for maintaining ethnicity shifts between an Hispano culture that anchors identity and an Hispano culture that holds back change. Where one places ethnic boundaries contributes to one's notion of the school's role in the community.

A FITTING SCHOOL FOR NORTEÑO

In Northern New Mexico, the essence of the Hispano experience emerges from the continuous reblending of tradition and change. Whether one perceives this reblending as strengthening or unraveling the social fabric depends on one's attitude about ethnic boundaries. The borderlands between Anglo and Hispano cultures offer choices that, depending on one's point of view, create tension or increase options for Norteño adolescents. In a school district ranked 10th poorest out of 89 statewide, the community is uncertain about who is responsible for helping children mediate between the complex worlds that encompass them. Norteños disagree about the social and cultural shaping of the young; they disagree on whether the schools should synthesize more than one cultural philosophy and lifestyle, or function with a preference for one culture or the other (Ramírez, 1983, cited in Rotheram-Borus, 1993).[19] Each approach puts a different emphasis on remaining and becoming. Each depicts a different role for Spanish culture and language in school life, and each results in a different outcome for the community.

Norteños disagree about which multicultural model holds the greater promise of sociocultural viability and educational equity. In the day-to-day life of Norteño, these models blend, while the cultural pendulum continues to swing. The myth of a bilingual handicap pressured children in the 1960s to feel ashamed of their own language and cultural background (Cummins, 1984): "Early interpretations of ... the minority experience assumed that living in two cultural worlds would result in intense conflict and confusion because of discrepancies between two competing cultural systems" (Rosenthal, 1987, p. 169). As grown-ups in the 1990s, some Norteño parents feel less successful without Spanish as the

---

[19]M. Ramírez outlined four different types of bicultural or multicultural identities in his studies about the personalities and mental health of Latin Americans: synthesized multiculturalism, functional multiculturalism with a mainstream orientation, functional multiculturalism with an ethnic group orientation, or mono-culturalism.

Anglo culture encroaches on the community. Indeed, the premiums offered by society are shifting the construction of ethnicity toward increased differentiation. Now it can be in one's best interest to
"dissimilate"—to assume cultural values and behaviors that distinguish
oneself from the dominant culture.

A generation gap exists in Norteño because young people have not experienced the same degree of rejection and conflict with the Anglo culture as their parents have: Most parents have a story of prejudice to tell,
and most children do not. Only those who have lived outside Norteño
know the rejection that accompanies being defined by others as the
wrong type of ethnic. Because most Norteño youth do not think of themselves in ethnic terms, they have not achieved the ethnic self-presenta-
tion of the adults. Few use ethnic self-labels; some refuse them.

Few Norteños advocate separatism in their everyday lives, but those
who support a stronger Hispano orientation in the schools are calling for
"double-consciousness"—seeking a voice that is expressed both individually and collectively, a voice that can speak in both the Hispano and Anglo worlds (Jaynest & Williams, 1989).[20] Those who prefer integration or
reform models fear

> one potentially paradoxical outcome of sustaining tradition and accommo-
> dating to social change: the stronger the core, the stronger the commu-
> nity; but the stronger the core and the community, the better it can resist
> change; and the better it can resist change, the more certainly it may resist
> learning how to accommodate change. (Peshkin, 1997, p. 52)

Ever since the Presbyterians opened the first plaza school in Norteño
in 1885, schools have been the site of a cultural battle over the minds and
faith of the young. The plaza school broke community patterns that re-
volved around family life, religious activity, and agricultural work. Education separated children from their parents and disrupted the
traditional ethnic socialization process. The Protestant notion of citizenship shifted the function of schooling away from religious teachings
and encouraged civic-mindedness directed toward state and nation.
Protestant concepts of determinism affected how Norteños see themselves in relation to their God. Secularization removed God's word from
the curriculum; standardization introduced foreign traditions.

---

[20]In *A Common Destiny: Blacks and American Society*, editors Gerald D. Jaynest and
Robin M. Williams (1989) used the concept of "double-consciousness" to look at the iden-
tity tensions created by the cultural duality of Black Americans who successfully seek the
American dream.

The forgotten people George Sanchez wrote about in the 1930s are no longer isolated, and time has tempered the rift between Protestants and Catholics. Norteño School District is run by Hispanos. School life is no longer alien to children, though it may remain so to grandparents. Individualism and material prosperity are common, and everyone agrees that education is essential to American life. But disagreement abounds over what interests should have priority. Supporters of bilingual education want to shift the Spanish language from the periphery to the core of schooling. To some, such a shift promises cultural autonomy, jobs, and resources; to others, it represents a return to isolation.

The staying power of Spanish American villages appears to reside in kinship, loyalty to community, attachment to the land, the comfort that comes from living among one's own, and the adaptive nature of the culture in the face of stress (Reich, 1979). Ties to people and place balance the forces that draw young people away from Norteño, and modest work opportunities and the welfare system allow some to remain in the community where their social network is strongest. Although most students view leaving the community as necessary for success, the legacy of family and land calls them back to visit or eventually to live there. As one middle-aged Norteño said while visiting for the annual fiesta, "Even though I left, I'm haunted by a desire to come back."

What kind of an education will bolster the community of Norteño as cultural crosscurrents alternatively shift talk to the utility of the past, the reality of the present, the promise of the future, and the prospects for cultural viability? Balancing the needs of the community with the welfare of the students requires a broad vision of the school–community relationship. If the community is viewed merely as the geographic location of the school, any good teacher will do. But if the community is viewed as the cultural context that distinguishes Norteño schools from others, who teaches and what is taught are critical decisions.

The intensity of the conflict in Norteño over the issue of bilingual education illustrates the intensity of identity politics in the area: "Many of those who defend bilingual education ... are not themselves comfortable speaking or reading the language, but that does not matter. The language is their flag, which they cannot surrender without giving up a part of themselves" (Fox, 1996, p. 237). The English language promises public individuality and access to economic life in the Anglo world. The Spanish language harbors Hispanos' private individuality, which is rooted in the ceremonies of community life in Northern New Mexico.

The debates about bilingual education overlap the earlier debates about secular education, community schools, and curriculum relevancy. When the Catholic religion and the Spanish language were removed from Norteño public schools, the rate of Anglo encroachment threatened to destroy Hispano culture. The community school approach of focusing the curriculum on local needs sparked disapproval and claims of Anglo colonialism. Is bilingual education the keystone for equity and achievement or for preserving language and culture?

Over time, changes in the structure of schooling have affected the structure of the bilingual education programs. Now the programs contain both transitional and language maintenance goals. Bilingual grant guidelines cause conflict: The incompatible goals of the transitional and maintenance bilingual programs in Norteño School District's K to 12 curriculum put teachers at odds with each other; short-term grants marginalize bilingual education; focus on remedial English diverts attention from educational inequities caused by poverty; dependence on external funding erodes local control.

There is no clear school policy in Norteño on whether to adopt a pluralist or assimilationist model of bilingual education. Both models begin with the premise that bilingual education equalizes and improves the teaching–learning environment for culturally diverse populations, but they differ in their long-term goals. The assimilationist model assumes that opportunities to study the history and culture of the ethnic group improve self-image, school achievement, and harmonious economic and cultural integration into the larger society. The pluralist model assumes that by including native language instruction and the study of history and culture associated with that language, bilingual programs have the potential to help maintain the community, cultivate positive ethnic group relations, and alleviate educational problems facing minority students (Pease-Alvarez & Hakuta, 1992; Trujillo, 1996).[21]

The Norteño school board's preference for hiring locals favors the pluralist model, but the model of an educated Norteño remains contested and unclear. Confusion surrounds critical issues: how to teach Spanish to students with a wide variety of Spanish language competencies, whether to

---

[21]Armando Trujillo (1996) analyzed the shift from a pluralist model to an assimilationist model of bilingual education in a Chicano-controlled school district in Texas. Trujillo explored how the model of a Chicano/a educated person became contested and modified. See "In Search of Aztlán: Movimiento Ideology and the Creation of a Chicano Worldview Through Schooling" in *The Cultural Production of the Educated Person* (Levinson, Foley, & Holland, 1996).

teach the colloquial Spanish, whether to make biliteracy a goal, and how to assess whether students move in and out of bilingual programs with success. Second- and third-generation bilinguals face complex challenges in preventing language loss, for they need to retrieve, acquire, and maintain language competencies (Valdés, 1997).

How much leeway can a school have in determining how best to meet the needs of its students? The case of Norteño illuminates how a public school tries to balance local and national interests. Catering to local identity may threaten national identity. Disagreement about who to hire reflects the tension the Norteño School District faces when deciding whose interests to serve and how. In the absence of a school district teaching ideology about culture, what is taught becomes a function of who the teachers are rather than a function of a culturally based educational process. A culturally based educational process is founded on traditional values, orientations, and principles while simultaneously using modern education's most appropriate concepts, technologies, and content (Cajete, 1994).[22] Such a process assumes that cultural nourishment transfers to extrinsic motivation. As long as the school district lacks reconciled policy and practice, community consensus, and a coordinated K to 12 curriculum for students lacking proficiency in English and Spanish, bilingual education is an uncertain keystone, vulnerable to political and financial quakes.

The ambiguity of finding a good fit between school and community underlies the ambiguity of remaining and becoming. As the form, viability, and cohesiveness of the community change in response to economic, political, religious, or demographic influences, what role should the school play in ensuring the survival of Norteño? For some, survival and self-determination come from cultural opposition—using the school as an ethnic boundary that perpetuates their unique language and lifestyles. They want the school to revitalize the community's capacity to coexist with the outside world by teaching students how to live well within their community. For others, survival and self-determination come from bicultural competence—using the school to prepare their children to compete in the outside world and using their knowledge of Anglo culture to benefit their own people (Rotheram & Phinney, 1987). In their view, the school should function both as mirror and window so they can see their own reality in relation to the realities of others (Style & McIntosh, 1988).

---

[22]In *Look to the Mountain: An Ecology of Indigenous Education*, Gregory Cajete (1994) promoted learning about life through participation and relationship in community. Cajete believes that every community must integrate modern education with the cultural bases of knowledge and value orientations essential to the community's way of life.

These roads to survival and self-determination reflect the bond rural people have with the places where they live. Both strategies acknowledge that education has been systematically stripped of its context and that, as a result, most people remain ignorant of the places they claim so proudly. Both strategies question whether Norteño students are learning how to live well in their own community or getting the impression that the good life can be lived only somewhere else. However, one strategy assumes that education is a process of trading ethnic self-awareness for things of lesser worth; the other assumes that education connects sense of place with a sense of civic involvement, worth, belonging, and becoming. Both strategies pose potential paradoxes: learning to become while still remaining; remaining different without marginalizing oneself.[23]

Norteños waged political war in the late 1920s to have an independent school district. Today's school district is the product of hard-fought battles between religious groups—Catholics and Protestants—and between villagers who promoted or resisted consolidation. In the 1990s, Norteño finds itself embroiled yet again in tension "between the fundamental promise of local control and the overwhelming reality of a national culture and economy" (Dunne, 1983, pp. 252–253). At a time when advocates for prescribed national standards are gaining momentum, citizens in Norteño are debating whether to provide a rigorous education that embraces, rather than rejects, their local culture.

The educators of Norteño are the "bridge generation" between how life was and how it is today in the village. Their different visions of the future put what to make of the past at stake. Most educators in the Norteño School District grew up speaking Spanish as their first language and being forced to speak only English in school. Few would dispute the socioeconomic gains obtained by this middle-aged generation through expanded schooling opportunities. However, now that the state has a favorable climate for bilingualism, Norteños have the opportunity to decide for themselves whether cultural or linguistic dualism is an advantage or disadvantage for students from Norteño. As Norteños continue to deliberate over their vision of an educated person, they will inevitably draw cultural boundaries that renegotiate the school district's teaching ideology and the process of asserting Hispano identity for succeeding generations.

---

[23]In *Place Value*, Toni Haas and Paul Nachtigal (1998), codirectors of the Annenberg Rural Challenge, questioned whether today's schools teach rural children to understand and respect their local history, landscape, and economy so that they can live well in their own communities.

References

Abel, Heather. (1997, June 23). A fruit-grower opposes mining—and tourism. *High Country News*, p. 9.

Acuña, Rodolfo. (1988). *Occupied America: A history of Chicanos* (3rd ed.). New York: HarperCollins.

Alvarez, Rosa Elvira. (1971, January). Chicano. *Chicanismo*, p. 11.

Anaya, Rudolfo. (1993, Winter). Mythical dimensions/political reality. *arellano*, 12–13.

Andersson, Theodore. (1973). Bilingual education: The American experience. In *Topics on bilingual-bicultural education* (pp. 4–20). Santa Fe, NM: State Department of Education. (Reprinted from the November 1971 issue of the Modern Language Journal)

Anzaldúa, Gloria. (1987). *Borderlands, la frontera: The new mestiza*. San Francisco: Spinsters/Aunt Lute.

Anzaldúa, Gloria. (1992, September). *The stories of multiculturalism*. A keynote address at the conference "Many Voices—Many Choices," University of Northern Colorado, Greeley, CO.

Anzaldúa, Gloria. (1999, October). *Nos/ostros: "Us" vs. "them," (des) conocimientos y compromisos*. A keynote address at the conference "Territories and Boundaries: Geographies of Latinidad," University of Illinois, Urbana, IL.

Archdiocese of Santa Fe. (1975). *50 years of love praise and service*. Santa Fe, NM: Author.

Arensberg, Conrad M., & Kimball, Solon T. (1972). *Culture and community*. Gloucester, MA: Peter Smith. (Reprinted from 1965, New York: Harcourt Brace)

Atencio, Paulette, & Cobos, Rubén. (1991). *Cuentos from my childhood: Legends and folktales of Northern New Mexico*. Santa Fe, NM: Museum of New Mexico.

Atkins, Jane C. (1982). *Who will educate: The schooling question in Territorial New Mexico, 1846–1911* (Doctoral dissertation, University of New Mexico, 1982).

Bachelor, David L. (1990). *Educational reform in New Mexico: Tireman, San José, and Nambé*. Albuquerque, NM: University of New Mexico Press.

"Back to School" Institute. (1992, September 19). Las Vegas, NM: New Mexico Highlands University.

Banker, Mark T. (1993). *Presbyterian missions and cultural interaction in the Far Southwest, 1850–1950*. Urbana, IL: University of Illinois Press.

Barber, Ruth K., & Agnew, Edith J. (1981). *Sowers went forth: The story of Presbyterian missions in New Mexico and Southern Colorado*. Albuquerque, NM: Menaul Historical Library of the Southwest.

143

Barring of nuns upheld in New Mexico school rift. (1951, September 26). *The Christian Science Monitor*, p. 8.

Barth, Frederik. (Ed.). (1969). *Ethnic groups and boundaries: The social organization of culture difference*. Boston: Little, Brown.

Bilingual ed. revives a threatened culture (1993, May 1). *The Albuquerque Journal*, p. A6.

Bodio, Stephen. (1990). *Querencia*. Livingston, MT: Clark City Press.

Borgrink, Henry. (1992). *New Mexico school district and school achievement profiles*. Santa Fe, NM: State Department of Education.

Brackenridge, R. Douglas, & García-Treto, Francisco. (1974). *Iglesia Presbiteriana: A history of Presbyterians and Mexican Americans in the Southwest*. San Antonio, TX: Trinity University Press.

Briggs, Charles. (1981). *'Our strength is the land': The Structure of hierarchy and equality and the pragmatics of discourse in Hispano (Spanish-American) 'talk about the past'* (Doctoral dissertation, University of Chicago, 1981). *American Doctoral Dissertations, 0215*.

Burciaga, José Antonio. (1993). *Drink cultura: Chicanismo*. Santa Barbara, CA: Joshua Odell.

Bureau of Business and Economic Research. (1992). *The census in New Mexico*. Albuquerque: University of New Mexico.

Bustamante, Adrian Herminio. (1982). *Los Hispanos: Ethnicity and social change in New Mexico* (Doctoral dissertation, University of New Mexico, 1982).

Cajete, Gregory. (1994). *Look to the mountain: An ecology of indigenous education*. Durango, CO: Kivakí Press.

Carlson, Alvar W. (1990). *The Spanish-American homeland: Four centuries in New Mexico's Río Arriba*. Baltimore: Johns Hopkins University Press.

Campa, Arthur. (1977). The Spanish language in the Southwest. In Américo Paredes (Ed.), *Humanidad: Essays in honor of George I. Sanchez* (pp. 19–40). Los Angeles: University of California Chicano Studies Center.

Campa, Arthur. (1979). *Hispanic culture in the Southwest*. Norman, OK: Oklahoma University Press.

Carter, Thomas. (1970). *Mexican Americans in school: A history of educational neglect*. New York: College Entrance Examination Board.

Chavarria, Jesus. (1977). On Chicano history: In memoriam, George I. Sanchez 1906–1972. In Américo Paredes (Ed.), *Humanidad: Essays in honor of George I. Sanchez* (pp. 41–57). Los Angeles: University of California Chicano Studies Center.

Cleric garb banned: 'Dixon Case' ruling tamed. (1951, September 20). *The Santa Fe New Mexican*, p. 1.

Cobos, Rubén. (1983). *A dictionary of New Mexico and Southern Colorado Spanish*. Santa Fe, NM: Museum of New Mexico Press.

Cobos, Rubén. (1985). *Refranes: Southwestern Spanish proverbs*. Santa Fe, NM: Museum of New Mexico Press.

Coffey, Amanda, & Atkinson, Paul. (1996). *Making sense of qualitative data: Complementary research strategies*. Thousand Oaks, CA: Sage.

Colombi, M. Cecilia, & Alarcón, Francisco X. (Eds.). (1997). *La enseñanza del español a hispanohablantes: Praxis y teoría*. Boston: Houghton Mifflin.

Committee for Consolidation. (1950). *Findings of the committee for consolidation at Norteño*. Norteño School District.

Constitution of the state of New Mexico. 1987. As adopted 21 January 1911, and as Subsequently Amended by the People in the General and Special Elections 1912 through 1986. Santa Fe, NM: Secretary of State.

Córdova, Gilberto Benito. (1979). *Missionization and hispanicization of Santo Tomas Apostol de Abiquiu, 1750–1770.* (Doctoral dissertation, University of New Mexico, 1979). *American Doctoral Dissertations, 0215.*

Córdova, Josephine M. (1976). *No lloro pero me acuerdo* (Kathryn M. Córdova, Ed.). Dallas, TX: Taylor.

Courts, Patrick L. (1997). *Multicultural literacies: Dialect, discourse, and diversity.* New York: Peter Lang.

Crawford, James. (1991). *Bilingual education: History, politics, theory, and practice.* Los Angeles: Bilingual Educational Services. (Original work published 1989)

Crawford, Stanley. (1988). *Mayordomo.* Albuquerque, NM: University of New Mexico Press.

Cummins, James. (1984). *Bilingualism and special education: Issues in assessment and pedagogy.* San Diego, CA: College-Hill Press.

Davidson, Ann Locke, Yu, Hanh Cao, & Phelan, Patricia. (1993, Winter). The ebb and flow of ethnicity: Constructing identity in varied school settings. *Educational Foundations,* 65–87.

deBuys, William. (1985). *Enchantment and exploitation: The life and hard times of a New Mexico mountain range.* Albuquerque, NM: University of New Mexico Press.

Delgado-Gaitan, Concha. (1994). Consejos: The power of cultural narratives. *Anthropology and Education Quarterly, 25,* 298–316.

Deutsch, Sarah. (1987). *No separate refuge: Culture, class, and gender on an Anglo-Hispanic frontier in the American Southwest, 1880–1940.* New York: Oxford University Press.

Diamond, Jared. (1994). Stinking birds and burning books. *Natural History, 103*(2), 4–12.

Diaz-Guerrero, Rogelio. (1987). Historical sociocultural premises and ethnic socialization. In Jean S. Phinney & Mary Jane Rotheram (Eds.), *Children's ethnic socialization: Pluralism and development* (pp. 239–250). Newbury Park, CA: Sage.

Donato, Ruben. (1999). Hispano education and the implications of autonomy: Four school systems in Southern Colorado, 1920–1963. *Harvard Educational Review, 69*(2), 117–149.

DuBois, W. E. B. (1969). *The souls of Black folk.* New York: New American Library. (Original work published 1930)

Duke, Biddle. (1993, March 3). 'Throw up some dust' to save culture, Hispanics told. *The New Mexican,* p. A4.

Dunne, Faith. (1983, December). Good government vs. self-government: Educational control in rural America. *Phi Delta Kappan, 65,* 252–256.

Earle, Clifford. (1949). *Dixon, N.M.—Testing ground for democracy.* Philadelphia: Presbyterian Board of Christian Education.

Edmonson, Munro S. (1957). *Los Manitos: A study of institutional values.* New Orleans, LA: Tulane University Middle American Research Institute.

Education in New Mexico. (1893). Frank Reeves Collection, Center for Southwest Research, General Library, University of New Mexico.

Eisner, Eliot W. (1979). *The educational imagination.* New York: Macmillan.

Epstein, Noel. (1977). *Language, ethnicity, and the schools: Policy alternatives for bilingual-bicultural education.* Washington, DC: Institute for Educational Leadership.

Espinosa, Aurelio M. (1911). The Spanish language in New Mexico and Southern Colorado. *Historical Society of New Mexico No. 16* (May). Santa Fe, NM: New Mexican Printing Company.

Espinosa, Aurelio M. (1985). *The folklore of Spain in the American Southwest: Traditional Spanish folk literature in Northern New Mexico and Southern Colorado* (J. Manuel Espinosa, Ed.). Norman, OK: University of Oklahoma Press.

Fincher, E. B. (1974). *Spanish-Americans as a factor in New Mexico 1912–1950.* New York: Arno Press.

Forrest, Suzanne. (1989). *The preservation of the village: New Mexico's Hispanics and the New Deal.* Albuquerque, NM: University of New Mexico Press.

Fox, Geoffrey. (1996). *Hispanic nation: Culture, politics, and the constructing of identity.* Toronto, Canada: Carol.

Free Schools Committee. (n.d.). *Appeal for free schools: The Dixon Case continues* [Pamphlet]. Dixon, NM: Author.

Friedman, Marjorie. (1978). *An appraisal of the role of the public school as an acculturating agency of Mexican Americans in Texas, 1850–1968* (Doctoral dissertation, New York University, 1978). *Dissertation Abstracts International, 39,* No. 4A, 2117.

Gallegos, Bernardo Phillip. (1988). *Literacy, schooling, and society in colonial New Mexico: 1692–1821* (Doctoral dissertation, University of New Mexico, 1988). *Dissertation Abstracts International, 50,* No. 4A, 0983.

García, Nasario. (Ed.). (1992). *Abuelitos: Stories of the Rio Puerco Valley.* Albuquerque, NM: University of New Mexico Press.

García, Nasario. (1992, October). *Wildflower Festival.* Las Vegas, NM.

González, Nancie L. (1967). *The Spanish-Americans of New Mexico: A heritage of pride.* Albuquerque, NM: University of New Mexico Press.

González, Phillip B. (1985). *The protest function of Spanish-American identity in New Mexico* (Working Paper No. 111). Albuquerque: University of New Mexico, Southwest Hispanic Research Institute.

Gordon, Milton. (1964). *Assimilation in American life: The role of race, religion, and national origin.* New York: Oxford University Press.

Grant, Blanche. (1936). *Cities, towns and villages—[Norteño].* Works Progress Aadministration Report, New Mexico State Archives, Santa Fe.

Griego y Maestas, José, & Anaya, Rudolfo A. (1980). *Cuentos: Tales from the Hispanic Southwest.* Santa Fe, NM: Museum of New Mexico Press.

Griego-Jones, Toni. (1996). Reconstructing bilingual education from a multicultural perspective. In Carl A. Grant & Mary Louise Gomez (Eds.), *Making schooling multicultural: Campus and classroom* (pp. 111–131). Englewood Cliffs, NJ: Prentice-Hall.

Haas, Toni, & Nachtigal, Paul. (1998). *Place value.* Huntington, WV: Chapman.

Hakuta, Kenji. (1986). *Mirror of language: The debate on bilingualism.* New York: Basic Books.

Hall, Stuart. (1991). Ethnicity: Identity and difference. *Radical America, 23*(4), 9–20.

Hayes-Bautista, David E. (1974). *Becoming Chicano: A "dis-assimilation" theory of transformation of ethnic identity* (Doctoral dissertation, University of California San Francisco, 1974). *Dissertation Abstracts International, 34,* No. 8A, 5332.

Henze, Rosemary C., & Vanett, Lauren. (1993). To walk in two worlds—or more? Challenging a common metaphor of Native education. *Anthropology and Education Quarterly, 24*, 116–134.

Hernández, Hilda. (1989). *Multicultural education: A teacher's guide to content and process.* Columbus, OH: Merrill.

Interagency Council for Area Development Planning and the New Mexico State Planning Office. (1962). *Embudo: A pilot planning project for the Embudo watershed of New Mexico.* Santa Fe, NM: State Printing Office.

Isajiw, Wsevolod W. (1974). Definitions of ethnicity. *Ethnicity, 1*, 111–124.

Jaynest, Gerald D., & Williams, Robin M. (Eds.). (1989). *A common destiny: Blacks and American society.* Washington, DC: National Academy Press.

Jones, Clayton. (1993, December 8). Contest over Asia: Cultural crosscurrents buffet the Orient. *The Christian Science Monitor,* pp. 11–13.

Kane, Cheikh Hamidou. (1963). *Ambiguous adventure.* New York: Walker.

Kimball, Solon T., & Partridge, William L. (1979). *The craft of community study: Fieldwork dialogues.* Gainesville, FL: University Presses of Florida.

King, Robert D. (1997, April). Should English be the law? *The Atlantic Monthly, 279*(4), 55–64.

Kluckhohn, Florence R., & Strodtbeck, Fred L. (1961). *Variations in value orientations.* Evanston, IL: Row, Peterson.

Kutsche, Paul. (1979a). Atomism, factionalism and flexibility [Introduction]. In Paul Kutsche (Ed.), *The survival of Spanish American villages* (pp. 7–19). Colorado Springs, CO: Colorado College.

Kutsche, Paul. (Ed.). (1979b). *The survival of Spanish American villages.* Colorado Springs, CO: Colorado College.

Larson, Robert W. (1971). Statehood. In Richard N. Ellis (Ed.), *New Mexico past and present: A historical reader* (pp. 190–207). Albuquerque, NM: University of New Mexico Press.

Lavender, David. (1980). *The Southwest.* Albuquerque, NM: University of New Mexico Press.

Leibowitz, Arnold. (1985). The bilingual education act: A legislative analysis. In M. Barnett & C. Harrington (Eds.), *Race, sex, and national origin: Public attitudes of desegregation* (pp. 219–268). New York: AMS Press.

Levinson, Bradley, & Holland, Dorothy C. (1996). The cultural production of the educated person: An introduction. In B. A. Levinson, D. E. Foley, & D. C. Holland (Eds.), *The cultural production of the educated person* (pp. 1–54). Albany, NY: State University of New York Press.

Levinson, Bradley A., Foley, Douglas E., & Holland, Dorothy C. (Eds.). (1996). *The cultural production of the educated person.* Albany, NY: State University of New York Press.

Levis, Gladys. (1978). *Is there 'something wrong' with Pedregales? An ethnography of cultural double bind.* (Doctoral dissertation, Northwestern University, 1978). *Dissertation Abstracts International, 39*, No. 8A, 5016.

Lopez, Richard, & Samora, Julian. (1977). George Sanchez and testing. In Américo Paredes (Ed.), *Humanidad: Essays in honor of George I. Sanchez* (pp. 107–115). Los Angeles: University of California Chicano Studies Center.

Lusk, Georgia L. (1932). *Report of the state superintendent of public instruction: For the eleventh biennium period beginning July 1, 1930 and ending June 30, 1932.* Santa Fe, NM: State Department of Education.

Lusk, Georgia L. (1956). *Twenty-third biennial report of the superintendent of public instruction: For the biennium July 1, 1954 to June 30, 1956.* Santa Fe, NM: State Department of Education.

Manuel, Herschel. (1965). *Spanish-speaking children of the Southwest.* Austin, TX: University of Texas Press.

McFarland, Thomas. (1987). *Shapes of culture.* Iowa City, IA: University of Iowa Press.

McGroarty, Mary. (1992). The societal context of bilingual education. *Educational Researcher, 21*(2), 7–9, 24.

Meeker, Olinda A. (1917). The evolution of Allison-James School. *Home Mission Monthly* (November 1916–October 1917), *31*, 4–6. New York: Woman's Board of Home Missions of the Presbyterian Church in America.

Meier, Matt, & Rivera, Feliciano. (1972). *The Chicanos: The history of Mexican Americans.* New York: Hill & Wang.

Meinig, D. W. (1984). Commentary on Nostrand's "Hispanos" and their "Homeland": Rejoinder. *Annals of the Association of Geographers, 74*(1), 171.

Momaday, N. Scott. (1966). *House made of dawn.* New York: Harper and Row.

Mondragón, Roberto, & Roybal, Georgia. (1994, Spring). *La cultura nuestra:* Outline of our hispanic culture. *La Herencia del Norte: Our Past, Our Present, Our Future,* 6–7.

Mondragón-Valdez, María. (1992). Surviving in the 21st century: My dreams, hopes, wishes for the survival of the Río Arriba. *arellano, 1*(5), 18–19.

Moyers, Robert. (1941). *A history of education in New Mexico* (Doctoral dissertation, George Peabody College for Teachers, 1941). *American Doctoral Dissertations,* 0080.

Murillo, Nathan. (1977). The works of George I. Sanchez: An appreciation. In J. Martinez (Ed.), *Chicano psychology* (pp. 1–10). New York: Academic Press.

New Mexico State Department of Education. (1971). *New Mexico school district profile.* Santa Fe, NM: Author.

New Mexico State Department of Education. (1973). *Topics on bilingual-bicultural education.* Santa Fe, NM: Author.

New Mexico State Legislature. S. L. 106, 37th Leg., 2nd Sess. (1986).

Norman, Deborah Melendy. (1993, April). *Northern New Mexico: The role of religious belief in cultural preservation.* A presentation to the Independent Scholars Association, Chapel Hill, NC.

[Norteño] School District. (1950). *Findings of the committee for consolidation at [Norteño].*

[Norteño] School District. (1991). *Curriculum development proposal for Spanish I and Spanish II: Norteño Jr.–Sr. High School.*

[Norteño] School District. (1993). *Transitional bilingual education proposal narrative for Title VII math and science programs in grades 7–12.*

Nostrand, Richard L. (1992). *The Hispano homeland.* Norman, OK: University of Oklahoma Press.

Novak, Michael. (1993). *The Catholic ethic and the spirit of capitalism.* New York: The Free Press.

Nuns were pioneers in public schools. (1974, March 2). *The Albuquerque Tribune,* p. A3.

Oral history program examines impact of Los Alamos National Lab on *paisano*s: Land abandoned for lab security. (1993–1994, Winter). *arellano,* 15.

Ovando, Carlos J. (1999, April). *Bilingual education in the United States: Historical development and current issues.* Paper presented at the meeting of the American Educational Research Association, Montreal, Canada.

Padilla, Pat. (1994, Spring). Prosperity for posterity at Los Alamos National Laboratory. *La Herencia del Norte: Our Past, Our Present, Our Future,* 40–41.

Paredes, Américo. (1978). On ethnographic work among minority groups: A folklorist's perspective. In Américo Paredes (Ed.), *New Directions in Chicano Scholarship* (pp. 1–32). La Jolla, CA: UC-San Diego Chicano Studies Monograph Series.

Parker, Kathleen. (1993, May 8). Not just water in a ditch: New economy, growing cities threaten state's age-old acequias. *The New Mexican,* pp. A1–A2.

Pease-Alvarez, Lucinda, & Hakuta, Kenji. (1992). Enriching our views of bilingualism and bilingual education. *Educational Researcher, 21*(2), 4–6.

Peshkin, Alan. (1991). *The color of strangers, the color of friends: The play of ethnicity in school and community.* Chicago: University of Chicago Press.

Peshkin, Alan. (1992). The relationship between culture and curriculum: A many fitting thing. In Philip W. Jackson (Ed.), *The Handbook of Research on Curriculum* (pp. 248–267). New York: Macmillan.

Peshkin, Alan. (1997). *Places of memory: Whiteman's schools and Native American communities.* Mahwah, NJ: Lawrence Erlbaum Associates.

Peshkin, Alan. (2000). *Permissible advantage? The moral consequences of elite schooling.* Mahwah, NJ: Lawrence Erlbaum Associates.

Phelan, Patricia, Davidson, Ann Locke, & Yu, Hanh Cao. (1998). *Adolescents' worlds: Negotiating family, peers, and school.* New York: Teachers College Press.

Pugach, Marleen C. (1998). *On the border of opportunity: Education, community, and language at the U.S.–Mexico line.* Mahwah, NJ: Lawrence Erlbaum Associates.

Reeves, Richard. (1993, May 3). English secure as first language in U.S. *The Albuquerque Journal,* p. A8.

Reich, Alice. (1979). Spanish American village culture: Barrier to assimilation or integrative force? In Paul Kutsche (Ed.), *The survival of Spanish American villages* (pp. 107–113). Colorado Springs, CO: Colorado College.

Reid, J. T. (1946). *It happened in Taos.* Albuquerque, NM: University of New Mexico Press.

Reiter, David. (1963). Presbyterians at work long before organization of synod. *Presbyterian Peaks, 7*(1), 5–7.

Rodriguez, Richard. (1982). *Hunger of memory: The education of Richard Rodriguez.* Boston: David R. Godine.

Rodriguez, Robert. (1991, September 10). English-only drive called divisive. *The Albuquerque Journal,* p. D1.

Rodriguez, Sylvia. (1987). Land, water, and ethnic identity. In Charles L. Briggs & John R. Van Ness (Eds.), *Land, water, and culture: New perspectives on Hispanic land grants* (pp. 313–403). Albuquerque, NM: University of New Mexico Press.

Rodriguez, Sylvia. (1996). *The Matachines dance: Ritual symbolism and interethnic relations in the Upper Río Grande Valley.* Albuquerque, NM: University of New Mexico Press.

Romero, Orlando. (1992, January 22–28). History, myth, and the *mestizaje*. *Santa Fe Reporter*, p. 12.

Rosaldo, Renato. (1989). *Culture and truth: The remaking of social analysis.* Boston: Beacon Press.

Rose, Charles. (1950). *Twentieth biennial report of the superintendent of public instruction: For the biennium July 1, 1948 to June 30, 1950.* Santa Fe, NM: State Department of Education.

Rosenthal, Doreen A. (1987). Ethnic identity development in adolescents. In Jean S. Phinney & Mary Jane Rotheram (Eds.), *Children's ethnic socialization: Pluralism and development* (pp. 156–179). Newbury Park, CA: Sage.

Rotheram, Mary Jane, & Phinney, Jean S. (1987). Definitions and perspectives in the study of children's ethnic socialization [Introduction]. In Jean S. Phinney & Mary Jane Rotheram (Eds.), *Children's ethnic socialization: Pluralism and development* (pp. 10–28). Newbury Park, CA: Sage.

Rotheram-Borus, Mary Jane. (1993). Biculturalism among adolescents. In Martha E. Bernal & George P. Knight (Eds.), *Ethnic identity: Formation and transmission among Hispanics and other minorities* (pp. 81–102). New York: State University of New York Press.

Rural Schools of America Act, S. 1472, *93d* Cong., *1st* Sess. (1993).

Sagel, Jim. (1992). *Dancing to pay the light bill.* Santa Fe, NM: Red Crane Books.

Sanchez, George I. (1967). *Forgotten people: A study of New Mexicans.* Albuquerque, NM: Calvin Horn. (Original work published 1940)

Schroeder, Albert H. (1972). Rio Grande ethnohistory. In Alfonso Ortiz (Ed.), *New perspectives on the Pueblos* (pp. 41–70). Albuquerque, NM: University of New Mexico Press.

Schwind, Mona. (1991). *Period pieces: An account of the Grand Rapids Dominicans 1853–1966.* Grand Rapids, MI: West Michigan Printing.

Sleeter, Christine E., & Grant, Carl. (1988). *Making choices for multicultural education.* Englewood Cliffs, NJ: Merrill/Prentice-Hall.

Smith, Marshall S., O'Day, Jennifer, & Cohen, David K. (1990). National curriculum American style. *American Educator, 14*(4), 10–17, 40–47.

Spindler, George. (1982). *Doing the ethnography of schooling: Educational anthropology in action.* Prospect Heights, IL: Waveland Press.

Stegner, Wallace. (1992). *When the bluebird sings to the lemonade springs: Living and writing in the West.* New York: Penguin.

Stieber, Tamar. (1992, August 16). Angry campers. *The Albuquerque Journal,* pp. A18–A19.

Stoddard, Ellwyn. (1973). *Mexican Americans: Ethnic groups in comparative perspective.* Washington, DC: University Press of America.

Style, Emily, & McIntosh, Peggy. (1988). Curriculum as window and mirror. In Peggy McIntosh (Ed.), *Listening for all voices* (pp. 1–5). Summit, NJ: Oakknoll School Monograph.

Suit demands removal of nuns from public-school positions. (1948, March 10). *The Santa Fe New Mexican,* p. 1.

Taos County Project Staff. (1941). Minutes (June 13), Florence Ellis Collection, Center for Southwest Research, General Library, University of New Mexico.

Taos County Project Staff. (1942). Minutes (January 9), Florence Ellis Collection, Center for Southwest Research, General Library, University of New Mexico.

Teschner, Richard, Bills, Garland, & Craddock, Jerry R. (Eds.). (1975). *Spanish and English of United States Hispanos: A critical annotated, linguistic bibliography.* Arlington, VA: Center for Applied Linguistics.

Tireman, Lloyd, & Watson, Mary. (1943). *La comunidad: Report of the Nambé community school.* Albuquerque, NM: University of New Mexico Press.

Trujillo, Armando L. (1996). In search of Aztlán: Movimiento ideology and the creation of a Chicano worldview through schooling. In Bradley A. Levinson, Douglas E. Foley, & Dorothy C. Holland (Eds.), *The cultural production of the educated person* (pp. 119–149). Albany, NY: State University of New York Press.

Turner, Victor, & Bruner, Edward. (Eds.). (1986). *The anthropology of experience.* Urbana, IL: University of Illinois Press.

Ulibarri, Sabine R. (1973). Cultural heritage of the Southwest. In *Topics on bilingual-bicultural education* (pp. 1–3). Santa Fe, NM: State Department of Education.

Ulibarri, Sabine R. (1993). *Tierra amarilla: Stories of New Mexico/Cuentos of Nuevo Mexico.* Albuquerque, NM: University of New Mexico Press.

Unser, Don J. (1995). *Sabino's map: Life in Chimayó's old plaza.* Santa Fe, NM: Museum of New Mexico Press.

U.S. Department of Commerce. (1992a). *1990 census of general population characteristics, New Mexico.* Washington, DC: U.S. Government Printing Office.

U.S. Department of Commerce. (1992b). *1990 census of population and housing: Summary of social, economic, and housing characteristics of New Mexico.* Washington, DC: U.S. Government Printing Office.

Valdés, Guadalupe. (1981). Pedagogical implications of teaching Spanish to the Spanish-speaking in the U.S. In Guadalupe Valdés, Rodolfo García-Moya, & Anthony G. Lozano (Eds.), *Teaching Spanish to the Hispanic bilingual: Issues, aims, and methods* (pp. 3–20). New York: Teachers College Press.

Valdés, Guadalupe. (1996). *Con respecto: Bridging the distances between culturally diverse families and schools.* New York: Teachers College Press.

Valdés, Guadalupe. (1997). The teaching of Spanish to bilingual Spanish-speaking students: Outstanding issues and unanswered questions. In M. Cecilia Colombi & Francisco X. Alarcón (Eds.), *La enseñanza del español a hispanohablantes: Praxis y teoría* (pp. 8–44). Boston: Houghton Mifflin.

Van Ness, John R. (1987). *Hispanos: Ethnic identity in Cañones.* (Working Paper Series No. 20). Stanford, CA: Stanford University, Stanford Center for Chicano Research.

Vargas, Philip. (1991, April 25). Hispanics must learn English or fall further behind. *The Albuquerque Journal,* p. 9A.

Villaseñor, Victor. (1991). *Rain of gold.* Houston, TX: Arte Publico Press.

von Maltitz, Frances. (1975). *Living and learning in two languages: Bilingual-bicultural education in the United States.* NewYork: McGraw-Hill.

Wagner, Jonathan H. (1920). *Annual reports of the state superintendent of public instruction to the governor of New Mexico: For the years 1919–1920.* Santa Fe, NM: State Department of Education.

Walker, Randi Jones. (1991). *Protestantism in the Sangre de Cristos 1850–1920.* Albuquerque, NM: University of New Mexico Press.

Walsh, Mark. (1993, May 19). Pomp and circumstance … prayer: High Court's ruling fails to quell issue. *Education Week,* pp. 1, 20.

Walters, Laurel Shaper. (1994, March 28). States seek fairer school funding. *The Christian Science Monitor,* pp. 11–13.

Warren, Nancy Hunter. (1987). *Villages of Hispanic New Mexico.* Santa Fe, NM: School of American Research Press.

Weber, Kenneth R. (1979). Rural Hispanic village viability from an economic and historic perspective. In Paul Kutsche (Ed.), *The survival of Spanish American villages* (pp. 79–89). Colorado Springs, CO: Colorado College.

Weigle, Marta. (1976). *Brothers of light, brothers of blood.* Albuquerque, NM: University of New Mexico Press.

Weinberg, Meyer. (1977). *A chance to learn: The history of race and education in the United States.* Cambridge, England: Cambridge University Press.

Wiley, Tom. (1952). *Twenty-first biennial report of the superintendent of public instruction: For the biennium July 1, 1950 to June 30, 1952.* Santa Fe, NM: State Department of Education.

Wilson, Chris. (1997). *The myth of Santa Fe: Creating a modern regional tradition.* Albuquerque, NM: University of New Mexico Press.

Wolcott, Harry. (1987). The anthropology of learning. In George Spindler (Ed.), *Education and cultural process* (2nd ed., pp. 26–52). Prospect Heights, IL: Waveland Press.

Woodbridge, Hensley C. (Ed.). (1997). *Guide to reference works for the study of the Spanish language and literature and Spanish American literature* (2nd ed.). New York: The Modern Language Association of America.

Yinger, J. Milton. (1981). Toward a theory of assimilation and dissimilation. *Ethnic and Racial Studies, 4*(3), 249–264.

Yzaguirre, Raul. (1998, August 5). What's wrong with bilingual education? Is it 'lingual,' or is it 'education'? *Education Week,* p. 72.

Zellers et al. v. Huff et al., 5332 N. Mex. 501 (1951).

Appendix

Population Decline of Hispano Villages
1900–1980

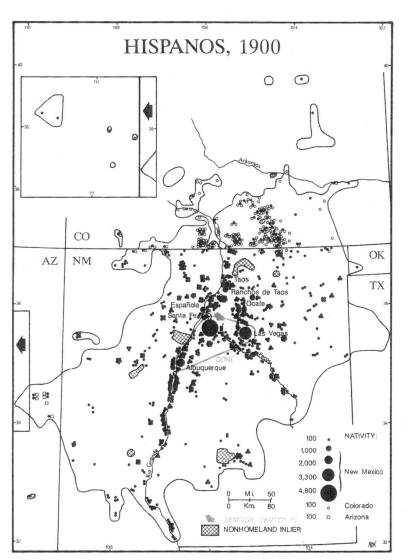

From *The Hispano Homeland* (pp. 207, 210), by R. L. Nostrand, 1992, Norman, OK: University of Oklahoma Press. Copyright © 1992 by University of Oklahoma Press. Reprinted with permission.

153

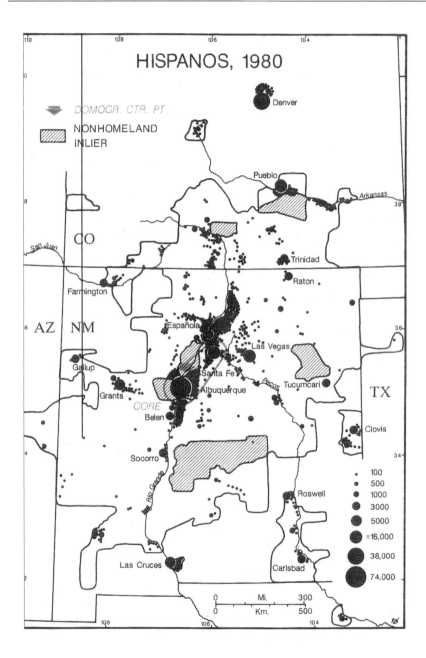

HISPANOS, 1980

Author Index

A

Abel, Heather, 127, *143*
Acuna, Rodolfo, 19, 32, 35, 54n, 123, *143*
Agnew, Edith J., 35, 36n, *143*
Alarcon, Francisco X., 65, *144*
Alvarez, Rosa E., 19, *143*
Anaya, Rudolfo, 51, 85n, *143, 146*
Andersson, Theodore, 124, *143*
Anzaldua, Gloria, 7, 20, 118, *143*
Arensberg, Conrad, 83, *143*
Atencio, Paulette, 85n, *143*
Atkins, Jane C., 34, 35, 40, *143*
Atkinson, Paul, 73, *144*

B

Bachelor, David L., 41, 132, 132n, *143*
Banker, Mark T., 36n, *143*
Barber, Ruth K., 35, 36n, *143*
Barth, Frederik, 136n, *144*
Bodio, Stephen, 127n, *144*
Borgrink, Henry, 24, *144*
Brackenridge, Douglas, R., 36n, 37, *144*
Briggs, Charles, 83, 84, 85, *144*
Bruner, Edward, 7, *151*
Burciaga, Jose Antonio, 72, *144*
Bustamante, Adrian Herminio, 2, 17, 18, 19, 20, 33, *144*

C

Cajete, Gregory, 141, *144*
Carlson, Alvar W., 20, *144*
Campa, Arthur, 17, 18, 19, *144*
Carter, Thomas, 41n, 123, *144*
Chavarria, Jesus, 121, *144*
Cobos, Ruben, 9, 21, 85n, *143, 144*
Coffey, Amanda, 73, *144*
Cohen, David K., 129, *150*
Colombi, M. Cecilia, 65, *144*
Cordova, Gilberto Benito, 73, *145*
Cordova, Josephine M., 18, *145*
Courts, Patrick L., 86, *145*
Craddock, Jerry R., 21, *151*
Crawford, James, 119, 124, 125, 126, *145*
Crawford, Stanley, 14, *145*
Cummins, James, 137, *145*

D

Davidson, Ann Locke, 10, 70, 137, *145, 149*
deBuys, William, 29, *145*
Delgado-Gaitan, Concha, 73, *145*
Deutsch, Sarah, 16, 18, 38, 120, *145*
Diamond, Jared, 84n, *145*
Diaz-Guerrero, Rogelio, 135n, *145*
Donato, Ruben, 3, 19, *145*
DuBois, W. E. B., 3, *145*
Duke, Biddle, 51, *145*
Dunne, Faith, 129, 132, 142, *145*

E

Earle, Clifford, 44, 45, *145*
Edmonson, Munro S., 84n, *145*

Eisner, Eliot W., 112, *146*
Epstein, Noel, 125, *146*
Espinosa, Aurelio M., 85n, 127n, *146*

F

Fincher, E. B., 122, 123, *146*
Foley, Douglas E., 140, *147*
Forrest, Suzanne, 32, 133, *146*
Fox, Geoffrey, 20, 21, 139, *146*
Friedman, Marjorie, 133, *146*

G

Gallegos, Bernardo Phillip, 2, 29, *146*
Garcia, Nasario, 127, *146*
Garcia-Treto, Francisco, 36n, 37, *144*
Gonzalez, Nancie L., 31, *146*
Gonzalez, Philip B., 18, 19, *146*
Gordon, Milton, 109, *146*
Grant, Carl, 112, *150*
Griego-Jones, Toni, 112, 119, *146*
Griego y Maestas, Jose, 85n, *146*

H

Haas, Toni, 142n, *146*
Hakuta, Kenji, 125, 126, 140, *146, 149*
Hall, Stuart, 86, *146*
Hayes-Bautista, David E., 69, *146*
Henze, Rosemary C., 113, *147*
Hernandez, Hilda, 114, 126, *147*
Holland, Dorothy C., 119, 140, *147*

I

Isajiw, Wsevolod W., 136, *147*

J

Jaynest, Gerald D., 138, *147*
Jones, Clayton, 109, *147*

K

Kane, Cheikh Hamidou, 3, *147*
Kimball, Solon T., 3, 83, *143, 147*
King, Robert D., 126, *147*

Kluckhohn, Florence R., 48, 118, 123, *147*
Kutsche, Paul, 116, 136n, *147*

L

Larson, Robert W., 33, *147*
Lavender, David, 31, *147*
Leibowitz, Arnold, 33, *147*
Levinson, Bradley, 119, 140, *147*
Levis, Gladys, 62, *147*
Lopez, Richard, 122, *147*
Lusk, Georgia L., 47n, *147*

M

Manuel, Herschel, 118, *148*
McFarland, Thomas, 84, *148*
McGroarty, Mary, 124, *148*
McIntosh, Peggy, 141, *150*
Meeker, Olinda A., 36, *148*
Meier, Matt, 119, *148*
Meinig, D.W., 21, *148*
Momaday, N. Scott, 69, *148*
Mondragon, Roberto, 94, *148*
Mondragon-Valdez, Maria, 128, 129, *148*
Moyers, Robert, 31, 32, 33, 44, 119, 120, 121, *148*
Murillo, Nathan, 122, *148*

N

Nachtigal, Paul, 142n, *146*
Norman, Deborah Melendy, 3, *148*
Nostrand, Richard L., 20, 136, *148*
Novak, Michael, 83, 148

O

O'Day, Jennifer, 129, *150*
Ovando, Carlos J., 119, *149*

P

Padilla, Pat, 5, *149*
Paredes, Americo, 5, *149*
Parker, Kathleen, 135, *149*

Partridge, William L., 3, *147*
Pease-Alvarez, Lucinda, 140, *149*
Peshkin, Alan, 3, 4, 70, 112, 112n, 113, 114, 138, *149*
Phelan, Patricia, 10, 70, 137, *145, 149*
Phinney, Jean S., 141, *150*
Pugach, Marleen C., 4, *149*

R

Reeves, Richard, 53, *149*
Reich, Alice, 139, *149*
Reid, J. T., 131n, *149*
Reiter, David, 30, *149*
Rivera, Feliciano, 119, *148*
Rodriguez, Richard, 87, 134, *149*
Rodriguez, Robert, 126, 128, *149*
Rodriguez, Sylvia, 133, *149*
Romero, Orlando, 20, *150*
Rosaldo, Renato, 7, 75, *150*
Rose, Charles, 47n, *150*
Rosenthal, Doreen A., 137, *150*
Rotheram, Mary Jane, 141, *150*
Rotheram-Borus, Mary Jane, 113, 137, *150*
Roybal, Georgia, 94, *148*

S

Sagel, Jim, 16, 127, 128, *150*
Sanchez, George I., 30, 121, *150*
Schroeder, Albert H., 29, *150*
Schwind, Mona, 42, *150*
Sleeter, Christine E., 112, *150*
Smith, Marshall S., 129, *150*
Spindler, George, 3, *150*
Stegner, Wallace, 134, 134n, 135, *150*
Stieber, Thomas, 129, *150*
Stoddard, Ellwyn, 18, 133, *150*
Style, Emily, 141, *150*
Samora, Julian, 122, *147*
Strodtbeck, Fred L., 48, 123, *147*

T

Teschner, Richard, 21, *151*
Tireman, Lloyd, 41n, 131, *151*
Trujillo, Armando L., 53, 54n, 114, 140, *151*
Turner, Victor, 7, *151*

U

Ulibarri, Sabine R., 50, 85n, *151*
Unser, Don J., 40, *151*

V

Valdes, Guadalupe, 65, 73, 141, *151*
Vanett, Lauren, 113, *147*
Van Ness, John R., 21, *151*
Vargas, Philip, 126, 127, *151*
Villasenor, Victor, 88, 89, *151*
von Maltitz, Frances, 124, *151*

W

Wagner, Jonathan H., 120, *151*
Walker, Randi Jones, 36n, *151*
Walsh, Mark, 25, *151*
Walters, Laurel Shaper, 130, *152*
Warren, Nancy Hunter, 17, 30, *152*
Watson, Mary, 41n, *151*
Weber, Kenneth R., 136, *152*
Weigle, Marta, 13n, *152*
Weinberg, Meyer, 32, *152*
Wiley, Tom, 46, 47n, *152*
Williams, Robin M., 138, *147*
Wilson, Chris, 18, *152*
Woolcot, Harry, 10, *152*

Y

Yinger, J. Milton, 12, *152*
Yu, Hanh Cao, 10, 70, 137, *145, 149*
Yzaguirre, Raul, 119, *152*

Subject Index

B

Becoming, 3, 7, 133, 137, 141
Bilingualism, 10–11, 15, 17, 27, 43,
    51–61, 63–64, 94, 111–112,
    130, 139–140
  debate among parents, 56–61
  debate among teachers, 52–56, 63,
    64
  students, 63–64

C

Catholic, 1, 13, 15, 25, 34–35, 38, 41,
    133
Competing local and national inter-
    ests, 129
  barriers to local control, 129–130
  community school concept,
    130–133

E

Ethnic labeling, 17–22, 35
  identity vs. identification, 69–72,
    133, 142
Ethnography, 3, 8
  Anglo, 3, 5–6, 12, 17, 27, 38, 51, 88,
    134–135
  Hispano, 3–6, 8–9, 26–27
  Indian, 3, 17, 133
  Mexican, 3

I

Intergenerational stories, 72–74
  multivocal story, 74
  Anaya narrative, 75–82

L

Language in schools, 119, 139
  advocacy for language-minority
    students, 123–125, 141
  contested rights about language,
    125–126, 141
  education inequality, 121–123, 139
  legislating language, 119–121, 141
Los Alamos, 4–6

M

Multiculturalism in schools, 118–119,
    137

N

Norteno, 1–6, 7, 12, 15, 38, 41, 56–61,
    133
  culture, 2, 4–7
  first mission teacher, 38–40
  public education, 2, 6, 9, 34–35,
    40–42
  religion, 3, 5, 16, 34–41, 42–49
    (See religion and schools)
Norteno educators' influence, 87–88,
    108–109

Alfonso: The importance of knowing two languages, 94
bilingual program, 94–97
Bolivar: Stand and deliver, 104–108
personal motivator, 105–108
Georgeann: The links of common knowledge, 92
current events and geography, 92–94
Hector: Leave to make something of yourself, 99–104
Kate: Where ethnic pride ends, 97–99
Luisa: The we of me, 88–91
challenges of the project, 91
oral history project, 88–90
Norteno ethnic identity, 133–137, 139–142
boundaries, 137–142
economic changes, 136
in-and-out migration, 136
land grants, 134–135
Norteno history, 1, 9, 13–17, 28
Mexican rule, 30–31
Spanish colonization, 28–30
U.S. occupation, 31–34
Norteno School District, 8–17, 23, 27–28, 51–52, 109–114, 142
community, 8, 10, 13–14, 23–25, 27, 60–61, 139
change, 9–10, 24–26, 62, 137
educators, 8, 10, 52–56, 87

ethnicity, 11–12, 59–60
students, 11, 13, 24–26, 27, 62, 87
teacher fit, 114–117
vocational training, 110–111
Northern New Mexico, 1–3, 50
Spanish culture, 50–51 (See Spanish culture)

P

Presbyterian schools, 35–38, 41, 138
Protestant, 1, 25, 35, 40, 43–44, 138

R

Religion and schools, 34–41, 42–49 (See Religion under Norteno)
Catholic public education, 42–49
Dixon case, 44–49
parochial schools, 45–49
Remaining, 3, 7, 133, 137, 141

S

Spanish culture, 62–69, 126–129
community, 84
crossculture, 63–64, 67–69, 83–86, 127–129, 139
Spanish language gap, 63–67, 84–85, 126–128
between generations, 65–67, 84–85